Fat Free 2

Fat Free 2

More Fat Free & Ultra Lowfat Recipes— No Butter, No Oil, No Margarine!

Doris Cross

PRIMA PUBLISHING

© 1996 by Doris Cross

PRIMA PUBLISHING and its colophon are trademarks of Prima Communications, Inc.

Library of Congress Cataloging-in-Publication Data

Cross, Doris.
   [More fat free & ultra low fat recipes from Doris' kitchen]
   Fat Free 2 / Doris Cross.
      p.   cm.
   Previously published in 1993 under the title: More fat free & ultra low fat recipes from Doris' kitchen.
   Includes index.
   ISBN 0-7615-0129-0
   1. Low-fat diet—Recipes.   I. Title.
RM237.7.C764   1995
641.5′638—dc20   93-23406
                                              CIP

95 96 97 98 99 AA 10 9 8 7 6 5 4 3 2 1

Printed in the United States of America

How to Order:
Single copies may be ordered from Prima Publishing, P.O. Box 1260BK, Rocklin, CA 95677; telephone (916) 632-4400. Quantity discounts are also available. On your letterhead, include information concerning the intended use of the books and the number of books you wish to purchase.

To Alice

TABLE OF CONTENTS

INTRODUCTION

I LOST 100 POUNDS . . .
I'VE KEPT IT OFF WITH
A LOWFAT DIET

Years ago I struggled with my weight and all the many health problems that go with being morbidly obese. After I lost 100 pounds, the big challenge lay before me—keeping it off! I chose lowfat eating because it fit my lifestyle, and I didn't have to give up delicious foods.

Diets that require drastic changes and strict, near-starvation guidelines just do not work! The secret to successful dieting is lifestyle change, and lowfat eating will fit how you live.

You may be considering a lowfat diet to lose weight, or because you are faced with health problems. Perhaps you are choosing to eat lowfat to avoid health problems in the future. Whatever your reason, I hope that you will discover through this cookbook how wonderful fat-free and ultra lowfat foods can taste. We're not talking about diet foods here just REAL food that tastes wonderful AND is lowfat!

Several years ago, I opened my own weight-loss center, guiding dieters on a lowfat eating plan. I began creating lowfat and fat-free recipes for my dieters, and the result was my first *Fat Free & Ultra Lowfat Recipes*. Since then, I have had the pleasure of hearing from many of you, either through letters or phone calls, or personally at some of my seminars. My greatest joy is to hear about the success you have had with my recipes, whether it is weight loss or improved health, or simply a recipe that you and your family enjoyed. The enthusiasm you have shown for my first book prompted me to write this one, and I hope it serves you well in your kitchens AND in your lives.

Sincerely,
Doris Cross

P.S. If you bought my first cookbook you will probably notice that I have used much more fresh garlic in this one. I have decided to include more fresh garlic because of the health benefits it might provide. You may substitute garlic powder if you wish, but I personally like the taste of fresh. If you've never used fresh garlic, buy yourself a garlic press and give it a try! Simply peel a clove, place it in the press, and squeeze. It's simple!

FAT FREE & ULTRA LOWFAT
SHOPPING GUIDE

Cabot Farms in Cabot, Vermont, makes the most heavenly cheddar cheese with only 2 grams of fat per ounce. Wonderful to just pick up and eat a chunk, it tastes like a full-fat cheddar cheese! This product also melts beautifully and grates nicely. To order by mail call (800) 639-3198. Ask for the 75% reduced fat cheddar.

Buttermist cooking spray is probably my favorite product, and something I use everyday. It has the same calories and grams of fat as other nonstick cooking sprays, except this one tastes like real butter! Spray it on toast, bagels, English muffins and popcorn. Bread items taste best if lightly sprayed before toasting. To order Buttermist on Visa or Mastercard call me: (405) 372-4105. To order by mail: Send check for $11.00 + $3.50 postage and handling for two 14-ounce cans to:

Doris' Diet Recipes
P.O. Box 549
Stillwater, OK 74076

Pioneer Low-Fat Biscuit Mix is a fabulous product with endless possibilities. It is made in San Antonio, Texas, and is only available on a regional basis. To inquire about availability in your area call (210) 227-1401.

Reames Free frozen homestyle noodles are fat free and delicious! The new No Yolk Noodles are also very good.

Louise's Fat-Free Potato Chips are brand new and should be on the market soon in your area. They have the crunch and taste of regular potato chips.

Healthy Choice Fat-Free Cheeses seem to be my favorites right now. Their Monterey Jack, which is delicious, has been temporarily removed from the market. According to the company, it is being reformulated and will be back on the shelves in the near future. **Kraft** and **Borden** also have great fat-free cheese slices.

Weight Watcher's has a new fat-free Parmesan cheese on the market that is wonderful. Look for it at your local store.

Land o' Lakes has the best fat-free sour cream, in my opinion. This should be widely available in supermarkets.

There are few brands of hot dogs that I would consider lowfat: **Healthy Choice**, **Hormel Light and Lean**, and **Oscar Meyer Healthy Favorites**. These have 1 or 2 grams of fat. Do not buy other hot dogs, such as those made with turkey or chicken. They are much too high in fat.

Turkey bacon is wonderful and has all sorts of possibilities, from bacon and tomato sandwiches to seasoning for other foods and dishes.

When buying tortillas, especially flour, be sure to read the label. Some have 1 or 2 grams of fat, while others have 5, 6, or 7 grams of fat.

Some honey mustards are fat free and some are high in fat. Read the label and be careful of any that list soybean oil as the first or second ingredient.

Most barbecue sauces, catsups, and mustards are fat free.

Rosarita now has canned no-fat refried beans. Great for burritos, dips, etc. Other refried beans have lard in them, especially the ones at restaurants.

Campbell's has done a great job of giving us some very lowfat condensed soups for casseroles and sauces. I'm hoping to see them do a 98% fat-free cream of celery in the near future.

Promise Ultra is a new nonfat margarine, which will satisfy some people who are craving butter. This is a spread only, and would NOT be a product you could cook or bake with.

Mrs. Butterworth's Fat Free Cinnamon Rolls can be found in the freezer section of most supermarkets. The rolls are ready to rise and then baked, and are yummy!

When buying salad dressing always read the back of the label, looking for zero grams of fat. Do not assume that "lite" or "light" or "low calorie" means fat free.

Entenmann's has brought us many delicious fat-free coffee cakes, cookies, muffins, and dessert cakes. The golden pound cake makes a wonderful base for berries, making it possible to have fat-free shortcake. Just remember these desserts are not calorie free, so enjoy in moderation!

Nabisco has done great things for us with their line of **SnackWell's** cookies and crackers. They are all very good now all they have to do is figure out how to make enough of the Devil's Food cookies to go around, since we all love them but can't find them!

If you are eating lowfat foods to lose weight, the lowfat cookies and desserts are marvelous alternatives to high-fat treats. Just remember that you cannot expect to lose weight if you eat unlimited amounts of something simply because it is fat free. Use moderation!

TIPS FOR SUCCESSFUL WEIGHT LOSS

Remember there are two things that contribute to successful weight loss: commitment and planning.

Have a plan and follow it exactly.

Do not diet or lose weight for someone else—do it for yourself. YOU DESERVE IT.

Be committed! No one can do this for you—you must do it for yourself.

Exercise daily, as permitted by your physician.

Eat a variety of foods. Do not eat the same foods every day.

Don't shop for groceries when you are hungry.

Carry fruit with you so that when you get hungry, you will have the proper food to eat.

Have raw vegetables prepared and in the refrigerator at all times.

When traveling, let a grocery store be your fast-food place. There are plenty of fresh fruits that you can grab and eat on the way.

The amount of fat in your diet determines the amount of fat on your body. Consequently, if you eat less each day than your body burns, the result is a slimmer you.

When eating chicken or turkey, always choose the white meat; the dark meat has more fat.

It is important on any weight-loss program to have a support system to help you and to encourage you on your way to your goal.

According to research, dieters who have some type of support system (spouse, counselor, etc.) lose 30% more weight than people who diet on their own.

Seek the support you need from a diet counselor, family and friends. Let them know how important this is to you.

Pay attention to emotional triggers that would cause you to eat something that is not on your weight-loss plan. Go for a walk instead of giving in to the urge to eat.

Try not to stay away from social functions because you are on a diet. Plan ahead and decide how you will handle the food that is going to be available; then go and enjoy yourself.

Dieting is hard work! It takes effort. Make a strong commitment to eat healthily; follow your plan and then enjoy the results.

There is NO magic diet or pill or plan to take weight off. It takes commitment and planning on your part.

Anything worth having is worth working for—this applies to weight loss as well. Give it all you've got.

Good Luck!

ACKNOWLEDGMENTS

The work of putting this cookbook together was made easier by many people. I gratefully acknowledge the willingness of family and friends to share their skills and ideas with me.

A special thank you to Jean Smith, of Tulsa, whose talents as a proofreader and typist played an important role in the completion of this book.

A very special thanks to my good friend Alice Shedrick for her neat ideas, cooking, and recipe testing. Thanks also for her writing skills and help with putting the final touches on this cookbook.

An equal amount of affectionate gratitude goes to my nephew, Greg Duckwall, for his great ideas, hard work, and his enthusiastic support to everything I do.

I owe my fondest thanks to Maurice Gershon, my good friend who continues to encourage and support me.

My sincere appreciation also goes to Mary Ann Grimsley and Deidre Warren, my two wonderful caterers. Their creative cooking skills and enthusiasm made recipe testing especially fun.

Also, Denise Luce and her husband, Marc, gave much of their time to this project by testing and tasting recipes. I am thankful for their interest and hard work.

A special thanks to Julie Finley, and all the girls at Genesis Beauty Salon for their taste-testing and critiques.

I also appreciate the willingness of Jeff, Sharon, and Abby Stokes to be enthusiastic tasters.

I especially want to thank my good friends Rick, Rodette, and Staci Green for their encouragement, ideas, and their tasting expertise.

Thanks to my sister, Marylin Nelson, for the hours she put in keeping my kitchen clean and running countless errands.*

A large and heartfelt thank you to Steve of Steve's Sundries & Books in Tulsa. His encouragement and willingness to share invaluable advice with me is a blessing.

I will always value and appreciate the advice and encouragement from my friend and lawyer, Michael Morgan.

I appreciate Tara Frick's willingness to edit and proofread, and I especially want to thank Hugh and Kathy Merrill for their computer knowledge and typing skills.

*In Loving Memory of My Sister
Marylin Jean Nelson
1937–1993

Fat Free 2

Fat Free 2

APPETIZERS, DIPS, & BREADS

Fat Free

BARBECUE WIENER TIDBITS
Delicious

1½ c. barbecue sauce
1   12-oz. jar grape jelly
8   fat-free hot dogs
1   green pepper, cut into chunks
1   medium onion, cut into chunks
1   15¼-oz. can pineapple chunks, drained

In large pot, combine barbecue sauce and jelly and stir with whisk over medium heat until jelly is dissolved and mixture begins to boil slightly.

Cut hot dogs into bite-sized pieces; add to barbecue sauce and simmer 5 minutes. Add green pepper and onion and simmer 5 more minutes. Add pineapple just before serving.

Recipe makes 8 servings.

Grams of Fat Per Serving	Calories Per Serving
0	236

Ultra Lowfat

GOURMET GARLIC BREAD
Great with salads and pastas

1 loaf fat-free, unsliced sourdough or French bread
$\frac{1}{2}$ c. fat-free mayonnaise
1 T. fat-free plain yogurt
1 T. garlic, chopped or pressed
$\frac{1}{2}$ c. fat-free Parmesan cheese or 1 c. fat-free
   cheddar cheese

Slice bread into $\frac{1}{4}$" thick slices. Place on ungreased cookie sheet.

Mix mayonnaise, yogurt, and garlic in small bowl until smooth. Spread over bread and sprinkle with Parmesan or cheddar cheese. Broil 5 minutes or until toasted. Great with basil sprinkled on top.

Recipe makes 16 servings.

Grams of Fat Per Serving	Calories Per Serving
Less than 1 gram	99

Recipe Contributed by: Jana R. Love, M.S.
Manager, Therapeutic Exercise Services
St. John Medical Center
Tulsa, Oklahoma

Fat Free

CREAMY HORSERADISH SPREAD FOR SANDWICHES
Just the right amount of zip

½ c. (4 oz.) Kraft fat-free cream cheese
½ c. fat-free mayonnaise
1 t. prepared horseradish
   dash of garlic salt
   dash of white pepper

In small bowl, stir cream cheese by hand. Add remaining ingredients and mix thoroughly. Chill and use as needed for sandwiches, etc.

Recipe makes 6–8 servings. Serving size is 2 tablespoons.

Grams of Fat Per Serving	Calories Per Serving
0	33

Fat Free

CREAMY HONEY-MUSTARD SPREAD FOR SANDWICHES
Yummy

½ c. (4 oz.) Kraft fat-free cream cheese
¼ c. Dijon mustard
⅓ c. honey

In small bowl, mix cream cheese by hand. Add remaining ingredients and stir. Chill and use as needed for sandwiches, etc.

Recipe makes 6 servings. Serving size is 2 tablespoons.

Grams of Fat Per Serving	Calories Per Serving
0	102

Fat Free

DIJON MAYONNAISE SPREAD
FOR SANDWICHES

1 c. fat-free mayonnaise
1 T. Dijon mustard
dash of garlic salt
dash of black pepper

In small bowl, mix all ingredients by hand. Chill and use as needed on sandwiches, etc.

Recipe makes 6–8 servings. Serving size is 2 table-spoons.

Grams of Fat Per Serving	Calories Per Serving
0	18

Ultra Lowfat

CREAM CHEESE SANDWICHES ON RYE PARTY BREAD

1   8-oz. can crushed pineapple, very well drained
1½   c. (12-oz.) Kraft fat-free cream cheese
2   T. green pepper, chopped
1   t. dry onion flakes
2   t. sugar
¼   t. seasoned salt (optional)
1   loaf sliced rye party bread

In medium bowl, combine all ingredients except bread and stir until well mixed. Chill well, then use as spread on party rye.

Recipe makes 10 servings.

Grams of Fat Per Serving	Calories Per Serving
1	123

Fat Free

GREEN CHILE QUESO

4   slices Kraft fat-free cheese
1   10-oz. can green chile enchilada sauce
½ c. stewed chopped tomatoes
1   4-oz. can chopped green chilies
2   t. dry onion flakes
1   clove garlic, pressed or ¼ t. garlic powder

In food processor, blend cheese and enchilada sauce until smooth. Combine with remaining ingredients and simmer in saucepan until heated. Serve warm with no-oil tortilla chips.

NOTE: Warm over very low heat. If heat is too high, cheese will separate and curdle.

Recipe makes 8 servings.

Grams of Fat Per Serving	Calories Per Serving
0	28

DAVID'S RANCH AND DILL PRETZELS

These make a great snack

1   18-oz. pkg. large broken pretzels
    Buttermist or any butter-flavored cooking spray
1   2-oz. pkg. dry ranch dressing mix
½   t. (approximately) garlic powder
2   t. (approximately) dill weed

Preheat Oven: 225°

Place broken pretzels in large bowl and spray lightly with Buttermist. Sprinkle lightly with ranch dressing mix, garlic powder, and dill weed. Toss and repeat 2 more times.

Pour on baking sheet sprayed with nonstick cooking spray and bake at 225° for 1 hour. Remove and cool. After thoroughly cooled, store in airtight container or resealable plastic bag.

Recipe makes 8 servings.

Grams of Fat Per Serving	Calories Per Serving
Less than 1 gram	239

Ultra Lowfat

GARLIC-CHEESE HOMESTYLE BISCUITS
Wonderful with my garlic butter

2   c. Pioneer Low-Fat Biscuit Mix*
¾ c. plus 1 T. evaporated skim milk
½ c. fat-free cheddar cheese, grated
     garlic salt to taste

Preheat Oven: 425°

In large bowl, combine biscuit mix, evaporated milk, cheese, and mix. Drop on baking sheet sprayed with nonstick cooking spray and sprinkle tops with garlic salt (should make 6 large biscuits). Bake at 425° for 10–12 minutes.

Recipe makes 6 biscuits.

*If you can't find Pioneer Low-Fat Biscuit Mix in your area, use a light biscuit mix; however, this will add a few grams of fat to each serving.

Grams of Fat Per Serving	Calories Per Serving
Less than 1 gram	251

Ultra Lowfat

CRISPY VEGGIE ROLLS
Like an egg roll—only better

14 egg roll wrappers

Filling:

1   10-oz. pkg. frozen corn, thawed
1   10-oz. pkg. frozen chopped broccoli, thawed
1   medium onion, chopped
4   T. (2 oz.) Kraft fat-free cream cheese
⅓ c. fat-free Parmesan cheese
1   T. Molly McButter
½ t. seasoned salt
     dash of garlic salt
     black pepper to taste

Dipping Sauce:

½ c. (4 oz.) Kraft fat-free cream cheese
1   c. fat-free sour cream
1   2-oz. pkg. dry ranch dressing mix

Preheat Oven: 350°

In large bowl, combine filling ingredients and stir with spoon until well blended. Place about ¼ cup filling in center of each egg roll wrapper. Fold wrappers according to package directions.

Place finished rolls on baking sheet sprayed with nonstick cooking spray, then spray tops lightly with nonstick spray. Bake at 350° for 25–30 minutes or until golden brown.

Prepare dipping sauce while rolls are baking. In food processor, combine all ingredients and process until smooth. Refrigerate until ready to serve with veggie rolls.

Recipe makes 14 rolls. Serving size is 2 rolls.

Grams of Fat Per Serving	Calories Per Serving
1	247

GARLIC BUTTER WITH FRESH BASIL
Wonderful on the garlic cheese biscuits

2 T. Molly McButter
1 T. Butter Buds
$\frac{1}{4}$ c. water
2 cloves garlic, pressed
few leaves of fresh basil (optional)

Combine all ingredients in small saucepan and heat 1–2 minutes over low heat. Remove from heat and serve.

Great on biscuits.

Recipe makes 3 servings.

Grams of Fat Per Serving	Calories Per Serving
0	18

Ultra Lowfat

CREAMY SOUTHWEST SOUP
Spicy—lots of flavor

2 slices turkey bacon, cut into small pieces
1 medium onion, chopped
1 14-oz. can chicken broth, defatted or fat free
2 16-oz. cans golden hominy, drained
2 c. water
1 4-oz. can chopped green chilies
1 clove garlic, pressed
   black pepper to taste
½ c. fat-free sour cream

Brown bacon and onion in large saucepan sprayed with nonstick cooking spray. Add all remaining ingredients except sour cream and simmer over medium heat about 20 minutes.

Stir in sour cream just before serving.

Recipe makes 6 servings.

Grams of Fat Per Serving	Calories Per Serving
1.5	156

Ultra Lowfat

WALNUT-RAISIN CREAM CHEESE
Try this spread on a cinnamon-raisin bagel

1½ c. (12-oz.) Kraft fat-free cream cheese
⅓ c. raisins
2 T. black walnut pieces, chopped fine
⅓ c. brown sugar

In medium bowl, combine ingredients and mix with electric mixer until sugar is dissolved.

This spreads better if refrigerated for a few hours after mixing.

Recipe makes 6 servings. Serving size is 2 table-spoons.

Grams of Fat Per Serving	Calories Per Serving
1.5	134

Ultra Lowfat

MEXICAN LAYERED DIP
A big hit for a party

1	lb. ground turkey breast or chicken breast
1	(1¼-oz.) pkg. dry taco seasoning
½	c. water
1	16-oz. can fat-free refried beans
1	4-oz. can chopped green chilies
1	small onion, chopped
1	c. fat-free sour cream
½	c. fat-free cheese, grated
1	large tomato, chopped (optional)

Brown meat in skillet sprayed with nonstick cooking spray. Add taco seasoning and water. Simmer and stir until all water is cooked away. Set aside to cool.

Spread refried beans evenly over bottom of 8" or 9" round or square baking dish. Layer with meat, green chilies, onion, and sour cream. Top with grated cheese and tomatoes. Chill and serve with no-oil tortilla chips.

Recipe makes 8 servings.

Grams of Fat Per Serving	Calories Per Serving
2	231

PARMESAN CHEESE POPCORN
Simple and fantastic

8–10 c. air-popped popcorn
    Buttermist (any butter-flavored cooking spray will
    work; however, I prefer the taste of Buttermist
    because it takes like real butter)
⅓   c. fat-free Parmesan cheese
    salt to taste (optional)

Lightly spray popped corn with Buttermist and immediately sprinkle on about 1 T. Parmesan. Toss popcorn
and repeat process.

BLACKENED PARMESAN CHEESE POPCORN
Hot and Spicy

Follow recipe above and add 1–2 t. blackened or
Cajun spices.

Recipe makes about 3 servings.

Grams of Fat Per Serving	Calories Per Serving
1	114

Ultra Lowfat

PARTY MIX
Great snack for the holidays

NOTE: You will need a small clean spray bottle

3 c. Rice Chex
3 c. Corn Chex
3 c. Cheerios
3 c. fat-free pretzels
    Worcestershire sauce
    Buttermist
    seasoned salt
    garlic powder
    onion powder (optional)

Preheat Oven: 200°

In large pan, combine dry cereals and pretzels. Pour Worcestershire in small spray bottle. Lightly spray top of cereal mixture with Worcestershire, then with Buttermist.

Lightly sprinkle mixture with seasoned salt, garlic powder, and onion powder. Stir and repeat this process several times. Be careful not to use too much seasoned salt, as it is very salty.

Bake at 200° for 1½ hours, stirring every 30 minutes. Allow to cool and store in air-tight container.

Recipe makes 6 servings.

Grams of Fat Per Serving	Calories Per Serving
1.5	256

HOLIDAY CORN BREAD DRESSING

Dry 7 slices of lowfat bread before preparing dressing.

Corn Bread for Dressing:

1¼ c. yellow cornmeal
⅓ c. sugar
¼ t. (heaping) salt
¼ t. baking soda
2 t. baking powder
1 egg white, slightly beaten
1¼ c. lowfat buttermilk

Preheat Oven: 400°

Combine dry corn bread ingredients and mix. Add egg white and buttermilk and mix. Pour into small square or round pan sprayed with nonstick cooking spray. Bake at 400° for 25–30 minutes. Cool and break into chunks.

Remaining Ingredients for Dressing:

1   medium onion, chopped
4   stalks celery, chopped
2   egg whites, slightly beaten
2   14-oz. cans low-sodium chicken broth, defatted
1½ t. rubbed sage
     salt and black pepper to taste

Preheat Oven: 350°

Simmer onion and celery in skillet sprayed with non-stick cooking spray until tender; set aside.

In large bowl, break up pieces of dried bread and corn bread and mix. Add onion and celery, egg whites, chicken broth, and sage. Mix thoroughly. Add salt and black pepper. Pour into 11" × 7" baking dish sprayed with nonstick cooking spray. Bake at 350° for 50–60 minutes or until golden brown on edges and top.

Recipe makes 8 servings.

Grams of Fat Per Serving	Calories Per Serving
1.5	216

Fat Free

SOUR CREAM, CHEESE, AND SPINACH DIP
Great with no-oil tortilla chips

1	c. fat-free sour cream
7	slices Kraft fat-free cheese
½	c. chicken broth, defatted
¼–½	t. seasoned salt
½	c. frozen chopped spinach, thawed, drained thoroughly
2–3	T. green chilies, chopped
2	t. dry onion flakes

In food processor, mix sour cream, cheese, chicken broth, and seasoned salt. Pour into small saucepan or very small crock pot and add spinach, green chilies, and onion flakes. Warm and serve.

Recipe makes 4 servings.

Grams of Fat Per Serving	Calories Per Serving
0	191

Ultra Lowfat

GARLIC TOAST
Fabulous—my favorite and so simple

1 loaf lowfat or fat-free sourdough bread, sliced
   Buttermist cooking spray or any butter-flavored
   spray
   garlic salt

Preheat Oven: 375°

Place slices of bread on cookie sheet sprayed with
Buttermist. Spray top of bread lightly with Buttermist.
Sprinkle lightly with garlic salt. Bake at 375° for
7–10 minutes or until golden brown.

Parmesan Cheese Toast:

Same as above, adding fat-free Parmesan cheese.

Ranch Parmesan Cheese Toast:

Same as above, omitting garlic salt and adding garlic
powder and dry ranch dressing mix.

Recipes makes 10 servings.

Grams of Fat Per Serving	Calories Per Serving
1 (Garlic Toast)	102

Fat Free

CUCUMBER AND GARLIC
CREAM CHEESE SPREAD

Fabulous flavor!

1	c. (8-oz.) carton fat-free cream cheese
2	T. cucumber, finely chopped
1	clove garlic, pressed
2	t. dry onion flakes
⅛–¼	t. seasoned salt, to taste

In small bowl, combine all ingredients and mix well.
Chill and serve on bagels or English muffins.

Recipe makes 8 servings.

Grams of Fat Per Serving	Calories Per Serving
0	28

Ultra Lowfat

HONEY MUSTARD
BAVARIAN PRETZELS

1 18-oz. pkg. large broken pretzels or 1 box large
      Bavarian pretzels, broken into chunks
¾ c. sweet mustard or honey mustard (find one that
      does not contain oil)
½ pkg. dry Hidden Valley Ranch Honey Dijon
      dressing mix
      Buttermist or butter-flavored cooking spray

Preheat Oven: 250°

Pour pretzels into large bowl and drizzle half the mustard over pretzels. Stir with large spoon and drizzle remaining mustard over pretzels. Stir again to distribute mustard.

Sprinkle with small amount of dry dressing mix and toss. Repeat until half the package is used. Spray lightly with Buttermist and toss. Repeat two more times.

Pour pretzels on baking sheet sprayed with Buttermist or nonstick cooking spray and bake at 250° for 1 hour, stirring every 20 minutes. Remove and cool.

Recipe makes 10 servings.

Grams of Fat Per Serving	Calories Per Serving
1	67

ORIENTAL MEATBALLS
Great for a party

Meatballs:

1   lb. ground chicken breast or turkey breast
1   8-oz. can crushed pineapple, drained
¾   c. cooked rice
1   egg white, slightly beaten
1   carrot, grated
⅓   c. bell pepper, chopped
1   T. lite soy sauce
2   t. dry onion flakes

Sweet and Sour Sauce:

1   18-oz. jar sweet orange marmalade
2   t. lite soy sauce
1   T. vinegar

Preheat Oven: 375°

Combine all ingredients for meatballs and form into 1" balls. Bake on baking sheet sprayed with nonstick cooking spray at 375° for 20 minutes or until brown.

In small bowl, combine all ingredients for sauce. Use as dip for meatballs or spoon over top when served.

Recipe makes 8 servings.

Grams of Fat Per Serving	Calories Per Serving
2	308

Ultra Lowfat

ARTICHOKE HEARTS
IN LEMON BUTTER SAUCE

1   14-oz. can artichoke hearts, packed in water
    juice from 1 lemon
2   cloves garlic, pressed
2   t. Molly McButter
⅓   lb. lite ham, shaved
¼   c. fat-free Parmesan cheese

Preheat Oven: 350°

Pour water off artichoke hearts and turn each upside down on paper towel to drain.

In small saucepan, combine lemon juice, garlic, and Molly McButter. Warm slightly and stir; set aside.

Choose small baking dish in which artichoke hearts will fit closely and stand up; spray with nonstick cooking spray. Cut ham in long strips and wrap each artichoke heart with 1 strip ham.

Place each wrapped artichoke standing up in baking dish. When all are wrapped and placed in dish, pour lemon juice mixture over top, filling each heart. Sprinkle with Parmesan and bake at 350° for 15–20 minutes. Serve warm.

Recipe makes 4 servings.

Grams of Fat Per Serving	Calories Per Serving
1.5	106

Fat Free

CREAM CHEESE PESTO WITH SUN-DRIED TOMATOES

Absolutely wonderful—great layered spread for parties

Cream Cheese Layer:

1½ c. (12-oz.) Kraft fat-free cream cheese
1 clove garlic, pressed
1 t. dry onion flakes

Combine ingredients and mix thoroughly.

Tomato Layer:

½ c. sun-dried tomatoes
2 c. boiling water

In small saucepan, cook tomatoes in boiling water 3–4 minutes. Set aside to cool; then drain. Process in food processor into small pieces; pour into small bowl and set aside.

Pesto Layer:

½   c. fat-free Parmesan cheese
2½ t. Molly McButter
½   c. fresh sweet basil leaves, chopped (measure
      before chopping)
2   T. chicken broth, defatted
1   clove garlic, pressed
    garlic salt

Combine ingredients and stir until thoroughly mixed.

In small bowl, spread thin layer of cream cheese mixture. Use all the tomato mixture for next layer. Gently drop and spread another layer of cream cheese mixture; then gently spread pesto over top. Add remaining cream cheese mixture for top layer and lightly sprinkle with garlic salt. Chill and serve with toast, bagels, crackers, or bagel chips.

Recipe makes 6 servings.

Grams of Fat Per Serving	Calories Per Serving
0	70

Ultra Lowfat

GOLDEN WAFFLES
A breakfast treat

1½ cups fat-free liquid egg product
1   c. fat-free cottage cheese
½   c. flour
¼   c. skim milk
1   t. Molly McButter
1   T. sugar
¼   t. salt

Combine ingredients in food processor and blend 1 minute. Cook on waffle iron sprayed with nonstick cooking spray according to waffle iron directions.

Recipe makes 6 large waffles.

Grams of Fat Per Serving	Calories Per Serving
1	70

Ultra Lowfat

HOMEMADE BAGEL CROUTONS
Great with soups and salads

2 bagels
   Buttermist nonstick cooking spray or butter-flavored
   nonstick cooking spray

Suggested various seasonings to sprinkle on:

Garlic powder
Garlic salt
Onion powder
Dry ranch dressing mix
Dill weed
Fat-free Parmesan cheese

Preheat Oven: 375°

Cut bagels into small pieces and spread on baking
sheet sprayed with nonstick cooking spray. Lightly
spray bagel pieces with Buttermist. Sprinkle on any
desired seasoning.

Bake at 375° for 5–12 minutes or until lightly browned.
Remove from oven and cool. Use in soups or salads.

Recipe makes 4 servings.

Grams of Fat Per Serving	Calories Per Serving
1	86

Ultra Lowfat

CORN BREAD ONION BAKE
Very good

Onion Mixture:

3 large sweet onions, sliced
1 t. garlic salt
¼ t. black pepper
1 c. (8-oz.) Kraft fat-free cream cheese

Preheat Oven: 400°

Brown and simmer onions until slightly limp in large skillet sprayed with nonstick cooking spray; season with garlic salt while browning. Remove from heat and add black pepper and cream cheese; set aside.

Corn Bread:

2½ c. lowfat buttermilk
½ c. sugar
½ t. salt
2 egg whites
2½ c. cornmeal
½ t. baking soda
1 T. baking powder
1 c. fat-free cheese, shredded

In large bowl, combine buttermilk, sugar, salt, and egg whites and mix with electric mixer. In another bowl, combine cornmeal, soda, and baking powder and mix thoroughly. Add to buttermilk mixture and mix. Fold in cheese.

Spread half the onion mixture in large casserole sprayed with nonstick cooking spray. Pour half the batter over onions. Repeat layers. Bake at 400° for 30–35 minutes.

Recipe makes 12 servings.

Grams of Fat Per Serving	Calories Per Serving
Less than 1 gram	188

DEVILED EGGS
No fat—no cholesterol; very good

5 hard-boiled eggs
1 c. fat-free liquid egg product
3 T. fat-free Miracle Whip
¼ t. horseradish
½ t. Grey Poupon mustard
½ t. vinegar
⅛ t. salt (optional)
   black pepper to taste
   paprika

NOTE: If you prefer a sweeter taste, use less mustard and add 1–2 tablespoons sweet pickle relish.

Cut hard-boiled eggs in half and discard yolks. Chill egg white halves while preparing filling.

Scramble egg product until done in skillet sprayed with nonstick cooking spray; set aside to cool.

Add scrambled eggs and all remaining ingredients except paprika to food processor and process until smooth. Fill egg white halves with mixture and sprinkle tops with paprika.

Recipe makes 10 deviled eggs.

Grams of Fat Per Serving	Calories Per Serving
0	26

Ultra Lowfat

ORANGE BREAKFAST ROLLS
These are fabulous

Rolls:

1   6-oz. can frozen orange juice concentrate, thawed
       grated peel from 1/2 orange
1   7 1/2-oz. can refrigerated biscuits (find one with
       1 gram fat per biscuit)
1/2 t. Molly McButter
1   T. sugar

Preheat Oven: 350°

Save 1 tablespoon orange juice concentrate for icing. Mix remaining concentrate with grated orange peel. Dip biscuits in concentrate and place in square or round baking dish sprayed with nonstick cooking spray. Sprinkle tops with Molly McButter and sugar. Bake at 350° for 30 minutes. Remove from oven and pour icing over hot rolls.

Icing:

3/4 c. powdered sugar
1/4 c. (2 oz.) Kraft fat-free cream cheese
1   T. orange juice concentrate
       grated peel from 1/2 orange
1/2 t. Molly McButter

Combine all ingredients and mix well.

Grams of Fat Per Serving	Calories Per Serving
1	155

Fat Free

CINNAMON ROLL-UPS
Easy and wonderful

Filling:

¾ c. applesauce
½ c. brown sugar
½ t. cinnamon
2   t. Molly McButter
    pinch of ground cloves

Topping:

¼ cup sugar
¼ t. cinnamon

8   egg roll wrappers

Preheat Oven: 375°

In small bowl, combine applesauce, brown sugar, ½ teaspoon cinnamon, Molly McButter, and cloves. In another small bowl, combine topping ingredients.

Place 1 egg roll wrapper at a time on dinner plate and spoon about 1½ tablespoons applesauce mixture over surface of wrapper. Start at one corner and roll up like a pencil, rolling on the diagonal. Finished roll will be about the size of a cigar.

Place finished rolls on baking sheet sprayed with non-stick cooking spray. Lightly spray tops with nonstick spray and sprinkle with sugar mixture. Bake at 375° for 15–18 minutes or until golden brown.

Recipe makes 8 servings.

Grams of Fat Per Serving	Calories Per Serving
0	117

Ultra Lowfat

FRENCH ONION SOUP
Great on a cold winter night

3   medium onions, sliced
1   T. flour
2   14-oz. cans Swanson beef broth, defatted
1   c. water
2   t. Molly McButter
¼   c. red cooking wine
½   t. salt (optional)
     black pepper to taste
6   slices sourdough bread, toasted
6   slices Borden's fat-free Swiss cheese

Preheat Oven: 375°

In large skillet sprayed with nonstick cooking spray, brown onions until golden brown. Sprinkle flour over onions and continue browning and stirring.

In medium saucepan, combine beef broth, water, Molly McButter, wine, salt, and black pepper. Add onions and simmer for 15–20 minutes.

Pour soup into individual bowls; top with 1 slice toast and 1 slice cheese. Warm at 375° until cheese starts to melt. Serve immediately.

Recipe makes 6 servings.

Grams of Fat Per Serving	Calories Per Serving
Less than 1 gram	167

CINNAMON PULL-APARTS

One of my best—don't miss it

Cinnamon Paste:

1   c. dark brown sugar
1   c. applesauce
2   t. cinnamon
    pinch of ground cloves

Sprinkle Mixture:

½   c. sugar
½   t. cinnamon

3   7½-oz. cans refrigerated biscuits (use fat-free or
        1 gram fat per biscuit)
2–3 T. Molly McButter

Preheat Oven: 350°

In small bowl, combine ingredients for cinnamon paste
and mix. In another small bowl, combine ingredients
for sprinkle mixture.

Spray bundt pan with nonstick cooking spray and sprinkle bottom with a little sprinkle mixture. Cut biscuits in half, dip in cinnamon paste, and cover bottom of pan with one layer. Sprinkle with a little sprinkle mixture and Molly McButter and repeat until all biscuits are used.

Bake at 350° for 30–40 minutes. Serve warm.

Recipe makes 10 servings.

Grams of Fat Per Serving	Calories Per Serving
2 (with 1 gram fat biscuit)	287

Fat Free

CLAM DIP

1   6-oz. can minced clams, drained
1½   c. (12-oz.) Kraft fat-free cream cheese
⅓   c. fat-free sour cream
5–6 drops Tabasco sauce
2   t. dry onion flakes
¼   t. garlic powder
½   t. seasoned salt (optional)
      dash of black pepper

Combine all ingredients and stir until thoroughly mixed. Chill and serve. Good with lowfat or fat-free crackers or pretzels.

Recipe makes 6 servings.

Grams of Fat Per Serving	Calories Per Serving
0	97

Fat Free

SPICY HOT BEAN DIP

1   16-oz. can fat-free refried beans
3   green onions, chopped
2   T. chopped green chilies
½   c. fat-free sour cream
½   c. fat-free cheese, shredded
2   t. dry taco seasoning
    sliced jalapeños (optional)

Preheat Oven: 350°

Combine all ingredients except jalapeños and mix.
Pour into small casserole sprayed with nonstick cooking spray and top with jalapeños. Warm at 350° for
20–25 minutes. Serve with no-oil tortilla chips.

Recipe makes 6 servings.

Grams of Fat Per Serving	Calories Per Serving
0	144

Ultra Lowfat

ORANGE RAISIN QUICK BREAD
Moist and delicious

1½ c. flour
1 t. baking soda
2 t. baking powder
¾ c. sugar
1 T. Molly McButter
⅓ c. fat-free liquid egg product
1¼ c. applesauce
    juice and grated peel from 1 orange
¾ c. raisins
1½ c. bran cereal

Preheat Oven: 325°

In large bowl, sift together flour, baking soda, baking powder, sugar, and Molly McButter.

In another bowl, combine egg product, applesauce, orange juice, and orange peel and mix with electric mixer. Stir in raisins and cereal.

Gradually add flour mixture to egg mixture and mix thoroughly. Pour into loaf pan sprayed with nonstick cooking spray and bake at 325° for 50–55 minutes.

Recipe makes 10 servings.

Grams of Fat Per Serving	Calories Per Serving
Less than 1 gram	214

Ultra Lowfat

CHICKEN PATÉ

Great on crackers for a party

4 boneless, skinless chicken breasts, cooked
1 egg white, hard-boiled and chopped (discard yolk)
1 small onion, chopped
1½ c. (6 oz.) fresh mushrooms, sliced and sautéed
½ c. (4 oz.) Kraft fat-free cream cheese
1 t. garlic salt
¼ t. black pepper

Cut chicken breasts into pieces and shred. Add remaining ingredients and mix thoroughly. Chill and serve.

Recipe makes 8 servings.

Grams of Fat Per Serving	Calories Per Serving
2	178

Ultra Lowfat

CHERRY BREAKFAST DANISH

$\frac{1}{3}$ c. fat-free cottage cheese
2 T. sugar
$\frac{1}{4}$ t. vanilla extract
1 raisin English muffin, halved and lightly toasted
2 T. cherry preserves

In small bowl, combine cottage cheese, sugar, and vanilla. Spoon over English muffin halves and top with preserves. Place under broiler until warm.

Recipe makes 1 serving.

Grams of Fat Per Serving	Calories Per Serving
1	411

Ultra Lowfat

BANANA BREAD

2   c. flour
1¼ c. sugar
1   t. baking soda
1   T. Molly McButter
⅓   c. light corn syrup
½   c. applesauce
½   c. fat-free liquid egg product
4   ripe bananas
1   t. vanilla extract

Preheat Oven: 350°

Combine all ingredients in large bowl and mix well. Bake in loaf pan sprayed with nonstick cooking spray at 350° for 50–60 minutes.

Recipe makes 10 servings.

Grams of Fat Per Serving	Calories Per Serving
Less than 1 gram	259

Ultra Lowfat

SWEET CORN BREAD

⅓ c. fat-free liquid egg product
1 c. evaporated skim milk
½ c. brown sugar
2 t. Molly McButter
1 t. salt
1¼ c. Pioneer Low-Fat Biscuit Mix*
¾ c. cornmeal

Preheat Oven: 400°

In large bowl, combine egg product, evaporated milk, and sugar. Add Molly McButter and salt and mix thoroughly. Add biscuit mix and cornmeal and stir. Bake in 9" square baking dish sprayed with nonstick cooking spray at 400° for 20–25 minutes or until golden brown.

Recipe makes 9 servings.

*If you can't find Pioneer Low-Fat Biscuit Mix in your area, use a light biscuit mix; however, this will add a few grams of fat to each serving.

Grams of Fat Per Serving	Calories Per Serving
Less than 1 gram	221

Fat Free 2

SOUPS, SALADS, & VEGETABLES

Fat Free

FANCY CORN
Delicious

1   10-oz. pkg. frozen corn
¾ c. (6-oz.) Kraft fat-free cream cheese
2   t. dry onion flakes
¼ t. garlic salt
2   t. Molly McButter
    black pepper to taste

Cook corn according to package directions and drain. Add remaining ingredients and stir over low heat 1–2 minutes. Serve.

Recipe makes 4 servings.

Grams of Fat Per Serving	Calories Per Serving
0	136

Fat Free

CREAMY GRAPEFRUIT–MANDARIN ORANGE SALAD

Nice combination of sweet and tart

1   16-oz. can grapefruit sections, drained
1   11-oz. can mandarin oranges, drained
½   c. (4 oz.) Kraft fat-free cream cheese
2   T. sugar
½   t. grated lemon peel

Combine drained fruit. In small bowl, combine remaining ingredients and stir until sugar is dissolved. Pour over fruit and toss. Chill and serve on lettuce leaf.

Recipe makes 4 servings.

Grams of Fat Per Serving	Calories Per Serving
0	150

Ultra Lowfat

SPAGHETTI SALAD I

1 10-oz. pkg. spaghetti, cooked and drained
4 slices turkey bacon, cooked and crumbled
1 c. chopped broccoli, lightly steamed
¾ c. chopped carrots, lightly steamed
½ 10-oz. pkg. frozen green peas
1 small purple onion, chopped
3 stalks celery, chopped
1 t. garlic salt
½ t. seasoned salt
1 16-oz. bottle Kraft fat-free Honey Dijon salad
   dressing

In large bowl, combine all ingredients except salad dressing. After all ingredients are mixed and tossed, add half bottle dressing and toss. Chill. Just before serving, add remaining dressing and mix.

Recipe makes 8 servings.

Grams of Fat Per Serving	Calories Per Serving
1.5	216

MAURICE'S CREAMY RASPBERRY JELL-O
Wonderful

1 3-oz. pkg. raspberry Jell-O
1 c. hot water
¾ c. fat-free sour cream
1 10-oz. pkg. frozen raspberries with sugar

Stir Jell-O into hot water until completely dissolved. Add sour cream and beat with electric mixer until smooth. Add frozen raspberries and blend in food processor. Pour into mold or bowl and chill until set.

Recipe makes 8 servings.

Grams of Fat Per Serving	Calories Per Serving
0	116

Recipe Contributed by: Maurice Gershon

Ultra Lowfat

PIMIENTO CHICKEN SALAD
Very good

Salad:

2 c. cooked white chicken chunks
1 small onion, chopped
1 stalk celery, chopped
2 T. chopped pimiento
1 apple, chopped
½ c. fat-free cheese, grated
   salt to taste

Dressing:

½ c. fat-free Miracle Whip
⅓ c. (3 oz.) fat-free cream cheese

In large bowl, combine salad ingredients. In small bowl, stir together dressing ingredients and mix until thoroughly blended. Pour dressing over salad and chill 1–2 hours before serving.

Recipe makes 6 servings.

Grams of Fat Per Serving	Calories Per Serving
1	114

Ultra Lowfat

CREAMED CORN CASSEROLE
Quick and easy

1   16-oz. can cream-style corn
½ c. fat-free liquid egg product
2   t. dry onion flakes
2   T. green pepper, finely chopped
1   t. Molly McButter
    salt and black pepper to taste
1   c. corn flakes, crushed

Preheat Oven: 350°

Combine corn, egg product, onion flakes, green pepper, Molly McButter, salt, and pepper. Pour into baking dish sprayed with nonstick cooking spray and top with crushed corn flakes. Bake at 350° for 50–55 minutes.

Recipe makes 4 servings.

Grams of Fat Per Serving	Calories Per Serving
1	125

Ultra Lowfat

BUTTERMILK COLESLAW

<u>Salad:</u>

6 c. shredded raw cabbage
½ medium green pepper, chopped fine
½ c. carrot, shredded
⅛ t. celery seed

<u>Dressing:</u>

1 c. fat-free mayonnaise
¾ c. lowfat buttermilk
¼ c. sugar
   salt to taste

In large bowl, mix cabbage, green pepper, carrot, and celery seed.

In small bowl, gradually add buttermilk to mayonnaise. Mix in sugar gradually. Add salt.

Stir dressing into cabbage mixture.

Recipe makes 8–10 servings.

Grams of Fat Per Serving	Calories Per Serving
Less than 1 gram	54

Ultra Lowfat

SUMMER PASTA SALAD
Wonderful unique flavor

Salad:

1   12-oz. pkg. tri-color rotella pasta
8   oz. boneless, skinless chicken breasts, cut into
      small pieces
½ t. garlic salt
      blackened or Cajun spices to taste
½ 10-oz. pkg. frozen Mandarin stir-fry vegetables

Dressing:

3   c. (24-oz.) Kraft fat-free cream cheese
2   cloves garlic, pressed
½ c. cucumber, chopped
¾ t. seasoned salt
2   t. dry onion flakes

Cook pasta according to package directions. Drain and rinse and set aside to cool.

Add chicken pieces to skillet sprayed with nonstick cooking spray. Season with garlic salt and blackened spices. Brown over medium heat until chicken is done. Set aside to cool.

In food processor, combine all ingredients for dressing.

Pour half the dressing over pasta. Add vegetables and chicken and toss. Refrigerate several hours. Add remaining dressing just before serving.

Recipe makes 6 large servings.

Grams of Fat Per Serving	Calories Per Serving
3	289

FRUIT SALAD DELUXE
Quick and delicious

1 15¼-oz. can pineapple chunks, drained
1 16-oz. can dark sweet pitted cherries, drained
1 11-oz. can mandarin oranges, drained
1 c. green seedless grapes
1 c. fat-free sour cream
½ c. sugar
½ t. vanilla extract
1 3-oz. pkg. dry banana instant pudding mix
2 c. miniature marshmallows

In large bowl, combine all fruit. With electric mixer, blend sour cream, sugar, and vanilla until sugar is dissolved. Pour over fruit and stir.

Stir in instant pudding mix and blend. Fold in marshmallows; chill and serve.

Recipe makes 8 servings.

Grams of Fat Per Serving	Calories Per Serving
0	248

Fat Free

CREAMY POTATOES

¾ c. (6 oz.) Kraft fat-free cream cheese
⅓ c. fat-free sour cream
¼ c. evaporated skim milk
⅓ c. plus 2 T. fat-free Parmesan cheese
3 large potatoes, sliced
1 small onion, chopped
  garlic salt
  black pepper to taste
  Molly McButter

Preheat Oven: 350°

In medium bowl, combine cream cheese, sour cream, evaporated milk, and ⅓ cup Parmesan and mix with electric mixer or food processor.

Line bottom of square casserole sprayed with nonstick cooking spray with layer of sliced potatoes and chopped onion. Sprinkle with garlic salt, black pepper, and Molly McButter and drizzle a little cream sauce over top.

Repeat with several more layers until dish is almost full, saving enough sauce to cover top. Sprinkle top with 2 T. Parmesan and Molly McButter; cover and bake at 350° for 1 hour.

Recipe makes 6 servings.

Grams of Fat Per Serving	Calories Per Serving
0	221

EGGPLANT CASSEROLE
Wonderful

1 medium-large eggplant, peeled and diced
1 t. salt
1 6-oz. box Kellogg's stuffing mix croutons
1 medium onion, chopped
⅓ c. fat-free Parmesan cheese
2 t. Molly McButter
¾ c. chicken broth, defatted
½ c. fat-free liquid egg product
   salt and black pepper to taste

Preheat Oven: 350°

Cover peeled and diced eggplant with water, add 1 teaspoon salt and simmer over low heat until tender, 10–15 minutes. Drain and set aside to cool.

Combine eggplant with remaining ingredients and mix. Pour into square or round baking dish sprayed with nonstick cooking spray and bake at 350° for 45–50 minutes.

Recipe makes 6 servings.

Grams of Fat Per Serving	Calories Per Serving
1.5	147

Fat Free

NO-OIL TABOULI

Try it—you'll be amazed!

1 8-oz. pkg. dry tabouli mix
1 c. cold water
1 cucumber, finely chopped
2 tomatoes, finely chopped
1 c. lemon juice
1 T. dry onion flakes
1 t. salt
1 t. black pepper
½ c. Good Seasons fat-free Italian dressing (mixed
       according to package directions, using red wine
       vinegar)

In large bowl, combine tabouli mix and cold water. Stir and let stand while preparing other ingredients.

Add remaining ingredients and mix. Let stand in refrigerator at least 4 hours before serving.

Recipe makes 10 servings.

Grams of Fat Per Serving	Calories Per Serving
0	63

HOMINY AND BLACK-EYED PEA CASSEROLE

½ can Campbell's creamy onion soup
¼ c. chicken broth, defatted
⅓ c. fat-free sour cream
¼ t. garlic powder
¼ t. chili powder
2 16-oz. cans golden hominy, drained
1 15-oz. can black-eyed peas, drained
   salt and black pepper to taste
½ c. fat-free cheese, grated

Preheat Oven: 350°

In large bowl, combine soup, chicken broth, sour cream, garlic powder, and chili powder; mix well. Add hominy and black-eyed peas and mix. Pour into casserole sprayed with nonstick cooking spray. Add salt and black pepper and top with grated cheese. Bake at 350° for 30 minutes.

Recipe makes 8 servings.

Grams of Fat Per Serving	Calories Per Serving
1.5	167

SPINACH CHEESE BAKE

½ c. frozen chopped spinach, thawed and drained
1¾ c. fat-free cottage cheese
½ c. fat-free sour cream
⅓ c. fat-free liquid egg product
2 t. dry onion flakes
2 T. flour
  salt and black pepper to taste
¼ c. plus 2 T. fat-free Parmesan cheese

Preheat Oven: 325°

In large bowl, combine all ingredients except 2 table-spoons Parmesan and stir with spoon. Pour into 8" or 9" square baking dish sprayed with nonstick cooking spray and sprinkle reserved Parmesan over top.

Bake at 325° for 30–40 minutes.

Recipe makes 6 servings.

Grams of Fat Per Serving	Calories Per Serving
Less than 1 gram	123

Ultra Lowfat

GREEN CHILE–ARTICHOKE BAKE

For artichoke lovers

2   14-oz. cans artichoke hearts
1   c. fat-free liquid egg product
½   c. evaporated skim milk
2   t. Molly McButter
2   T. flour
⅓   c. fat-free sour cream
1   4-oz. can chopped green chilies
2   t. dry onion flakes
⅓   c. fat-free cheese, grated
      salt and black pepper to taste

Preheat Oven: 350°

Drain artichoke hearts and cut into quarters.

In large bowl, combine egg product, evaporated milk, and Molly McButter, using electric mixer. Continue mixing and gradually add flour and then sour cream. Using spoon, stir in artichoke pieces, green chilies, onion flakes, and cheese. Add salt and black pepper.

Pour mixture into 9" casserole sprayed with nonstick cooking spray and bake at 350° for 45 minutes.

Recipe makes 6 servings.

Grams of Fat Per Serving	Calories Per Serving
Less than 1 gram	153

Fat Free

PEACHES AND CREAM GELATIN SALAD
Pretty salad—wonderful flavor

1 29-oz. can sliced peaches, drained (save juice)
½ c. (4 oz.) fat-free cream cheese
⅓ c. fat-free sour cream
¼ cup sugar
1 3-oz. pkg. peach-flavored gelatin

In food processor, combine ½ can drained peaches, cream cheese, sour cream, and sugar. Blend until smooth.

Add water to juice from peaches to make 1 cup and heat over medium heat until almost boiling. Remove from heat and add gelatin. Stir until dissolved. Cool slightly and combine with cream cheese mixture.

Add remaining peaches and pour into mold or dish and chill until set.

Recipe makes 6 servings.

Grams of Fat Per Serving	Calories Per Serving
0	113

Ultra Lowfat

BROCCOLI AND CHEESE SOUP

1   14-oz. can chicken broth, defatted
1   10-oz. pkg. frozen chopped broccoli
1   stalk celery, chopped
1   t. dry onion flakes
½   c. evaporated skim milk
1   T. Molly McButter
¼   c. fat-free sour cream
4   slices Kraft fat-free American cheese
    black pepper to taste

In medium saucepan, simmer chicken broth, broccoli, celery, and onion flakes 10 minutes. Add evaporated milk, Molly McButter, and sour cream. Simmer 1 minute. DO NOT BOIL.

Break cheese into small pieces and drop into soup. Stir and simmer until cheese melts. Add black pepper. Serve.

Recipe makes 4 servings.

Grams of Fat Per Serving	Calories Per Serving
Less than 1 gram	102

CORN CHIP POTATO SALAD
Delicious and different

Dressing:

½ c. fat-free mayonnaise
½ c. (4 oz.) Kraft fat-free cream cheese
½ t. spicy mustard
½ t. horseradish
1 clove garlic, pressed
¼ t. black pepper

Salad:

4 medium red potatoes, cooked and cubed
1 medium onion, chopped
⅓ c. green pepper, chopped
⅓ c. carrot, grated
⅓ c. celery, chopped
¾ c. crushed oil-free tortilla chips

In medium bowl, combine dressing ingredients and mix.

In large bowl, combine potatoes, onion, green pepper, carrot, and celery. Pour dressing over salad and toss. Refrigerate 2–3 hours before serving. Just before serving, sprinkle tortilla chips over each serving.

Recipe makes 6 servings.

Grams of Fat Per Serving	Calories Per Serving
Less than 1 gram	173

Ultra Lowfat

SALMON PASTA SALAD

4   c. cooked pasta
1   6$\frac{1}{8}$-oz. can salmon, drained
$\frac{1}{2}$ medium onion, chopped
$\frac{3}{4}$ c. chopped celery
$\frac{1}{2}$ red bell pepper, chopped
1   c. carrots, chopped and lightly steamed
1   t. dill weed
1   T. lemon juice
1$\frac{1}{2}$ c. fat-free ranch dressing

In large bowl, combine all ingredients except dressing and toss. Add half the dressing and toss. Chill and add remaining dressing just before serving.

Recipe makes 8 servings.

Grams of Fat Per Serving	Calories Per Serving
2	200

Ultra Lowfat

CREAMY OVEN HASH BROWNS
Complements any meal

1   10-oz. can Campbell's 97% fat-free cream of
      mushroom soup
1¼ c. chicken broth, defatted
½   c. fat-free sour cream
1   T. Molly McButter
      salt and black pepper to taste
1   24-oz. pkg. O'Brien frozen hash brown potatoes
      (with green peppers and onions)
½   c. fat-free Parmesan cheese

Preheat Oven: 350°

In large bowl, combine soup, chicken broth, sour
cream, Molly McButter, salt, and pepper; mix thoroughly. Add hash brown potatoes and mix.

Pour into 9" x 13" baking dish sprayed with nonstick
cooking spray. Sprinkle Parmesan on top and bake at
350° for 40–45 minutes.

Recipe makes 9 servings.

Grams of Fat Per Serving	Calories Per Serving
2	116

FANCY MASHED POTATOES

mashed potato flakes
1 T. Molly McButter
evaporated skim milk
2 slices turkey bacon, cooked and crumbled
⅓ c. fat-free sour cream
1 T. dry ranch dressing mix
1 green onion, sliced thin

Prepare mashed potatoes according to package directions for 4 servings. Omit butter or margarine and use Molly McButter. Use evaporated skim milk. Add bacon, sour cream, dressing mix, and onion. Mix thoroughly. Serve warm.

Recipe makes 4 servings.

Grams of Fat Per Serving	Calories Per Serving
1.5	147

Fat Free

ORANGE SWEET POTATO CASSEROLE
Especially for Greg

4   medium sweet potatoes, baked
3   T. orange juice concentrate
    grated peel from ½ orange
½ c. brown sugar
2   t. lemon juice
2   t. Molly McButter
2   c. miniature marshmallows

Preheat Oven: 350°

Remove skin from baked sweet potatoes and place in large bowl. Add orange juice concentrate, grated orange peel, brown sugar, lemon juice, and Molly McButter and mix. Fold in marshmallows. Bake in casserole sprayed with nonstick cooking spray at 350° for 25–35 minutes.

Recipe makes 6 servings.

Grams of Fat Per Serving	Calories Per Serving
0	179

Ultra Lowfat

OLD-FASHIONED BAKED BEANS

2   15-oz. cans pinto or navy beans, partially drained
½   c. dark brown sugar
⅓   c. ketchup
¼   t. liquid smoke
2   t. dry onion flakes
2   slices turkey bacon, cut in half

Preheat Oven: 350°

In large bowl, combine all ingredients except bacon and mix thoroughly. Pour into baking dish sprayed with nonstick cooking spray and lay bacon slices on top. Bake at 350° for 45–55 minutes.

Recipe makes 6 servings.

Grams of Fat Per Serving	Calories Per Serving
1	264

Ultra Lowfat

BLACK-EYED PEA AND CORN SALAD

Salad:

1   16-oz. can black-eyed peas, drained
1   16-oz. can whole-kernel corn, drained
1   14-oz. can artichoke hearts in water, drained and
      quartered
1   small onion, chopped
½ c. celery, chopped
½ small green pepper, chopped
    black pepper to taste

Dressing:

1   c. (8-oz.) Kraft fat-free cream cheese
½ t. horseradish
1   clove garlic, pressed
½ t. seasoned salt (optional)

In large bowl, combine salad ingredients. In small bowl, combine dressing ingredients and mix thoroughly. Pour over salad and chill several hours before serving.

Recipe makes 8 servings.

Grams of Fat Per Serving	Calories Per Serving
1	178

Ultra Lowfat

BEAN SALAD

Salad:

1   15-oz. can white beans, drained and rinsed
1   15-oz. can red kidney beans, drained and rinsed
1   small onion, chopped
½   c. chopped celery
½   bell pepper, chopped
½   medium cucumber, chopped
4   radishes, sliced

Dressing:

1   c. (8-oz.) Kraft fat-free cream cheese
1   T. tomato paste
¼   t. lite soy sauce
1   clove garlic, pressed
¼   t. seasoned salt (optional)

In large bowl, combine salad ingredients. In small bowl, combine dressing ingredients and pour over salad. Chill before serving.

Recipe makes 6 servings.

Grams of Fat Per Serving	Calories Per Serving
Less than 1 gram	211

Ultra Lowfat

SWEET POTATO FRENCH FRIES

A new twist on an old favorite

3 medium, fresh sweet potatoes
  Buttermist or other butter-flavored nonstick cooking
    spray
¼ c. sugar
½ t. cinnamon

Preheat Oven: 375°

Peel and slice sweet potatoes like French fries. Spread on baking sheet sprayed with nonstick cooking spray and lightly spray potatoes.

In small bowl, mix together sugar and cinnamon. Sprinkle over potatoes and bake at 375° for 20–25 minutes or until tender.

Alternate Seasoning: seasoned salt instead of sugar and cinnamon.

Recipe makes 3 servings.

Grams of Fat Per Serving	Calories Per Serving
1	185

Ultra Lowfat

STUFFED TOMATOES
These are great

4   large tomatoes
1¼ c. cooked rice
4   slices turkey bacon, cooked and crumbled
2   green onions, chopped
½   cup fat-free cheese, shredded
2   t. Molly McButter
5   drops Tabasco sauce
⅛   t. garlic powder
     salt and black pepper to taste

Preheat Oven: 350°

Slice top off each tomato and remove pulp. Combine remaining ingredients and mix well. Stuff tomatoes with rice mixture and bake in baking dish sprayed with nonstick cooking spray at 350° for 25 minutes.

These may also be served unbaked and chilled; however, I prefer them baked.

Recipe makes 4 servings.

Grams of Fat Per Serving	Calories Per Serving
2	138

Ultra Lowfat

JULIE'S POTATOES
Yummy

¾ c. fat-free sour cream
1 small onion, chopped
2 t. Molly McButter
⅓ c. light Cheez Whiz
4 large potatoes, thinly sliced
   salt and black pepper to taste
1 c. crushed corn flakes

Preheat Oven: 425°

In medium bowl, combine sour cream, onion, Molly McButter, and Cheez Whiz and stir with spoon. Pour over potatoes in large bowl and stir. Pour into square casserole sprayed with nonstick cooking spray. Add salt and pepper and bake at 425° for 1 hour. Top with corn flakes last 10 minutes.

Recipe makes 8 servings.

Grams of Fat Per Serving	Calories Per Serving
1	186

Recipe Contributed by: Julie Finley

Ultra Lowfat

CAJUN SEAFOOD SALAD
Spicy and refreshing

$\frac{1}{2}$ c. fat-free Italian dressing
1 T. spicy hot mustard
1 c. cooked shrimp or lobster pieces
2 c. cooked rice
6 green onions, chopped
2 stalks celery, chopped
2 T. dill pickle relish
2 T. sweet pickle relish
1 t. Louisiana hot sauce
$\frac{1}{2}$ t. seasoned salt
$\frac{1}{4}$ t. garlic salt

In small bowl, combine Italian dressing and mustard
and stir until blended. In large bowl, combine remaining ingredients. Add dressing; chill and serve.

Recipe makes 6 servings.

Grams of Fat Per Serving	Calories Per Serving
1	116

Fat Free

EGGPLANT PARMESAN

1 medium eggplant, peeled and sliced into $\frac{1}{2}$" slices
2 egg whites, slightly beaten
2 c. crushed corn flakes
$\frac{3}{4}$ c. fat-free Parmesan cheese
$\frac{1}{2}$ c. fat-free mozzarella cheese, shredded
1 can stewed chopped tomatoes
1 small onion, chopped
1 t. garlic powder
   black pepper to taste

Preheat Oven: 350°

Dip eggplant slices in egg white and roll in corn flakes. Brown lightly in skillet sprayed with nonstick cooking spray.

Place eggplant in large casserole sprayed with nonstick cooking spray. Sprinkle with Parmesan and mozzarella cheese. Gently pour tomatoes over entire casserole. Sprinkle onions over top and season with garlic powder and black pepper. Bake at 350° for 45–50 minutes.

Recipe makes 6 servings.

Grams of Fat Per Serving	Calories Per Serving
0	118

HOMINY CASSEROLE

2 16-oz. cans hominy
1 small onion, chopped
1 4-oz. jar chopped pimientos
1 10-oz. can Campbell's 97% fat-free cream of
    mushroom soup
1 4-oz. can sliced mushrooms, drained
½ c. chicken broth, defatted
½ c. fat-free sour cream
1 T. Molly McButter
½ c. fat-free mozzarella cheese, shredded
    salt and black pepper to taste
½ c. crushed corn flakes

Preheat Oven: 350°

Combine all ingredients except corn flakes and mix
thoroughly. Pour into small casserole sprayed with
nonstick cooking spray. Top with crushed corn flakes
and bake at 350° for 35–45 minutes.

Recipe makes 8 servings.

Grams of Fat Per Serving	Calories Per Serving
1	139

Ultra Lowfat

LAYERED PEA SALAD

1½ c. fat-free cottage cheese
3   c. lettuce, shredded
1   16-oz. can black-eyed peas
1   c. shredded fat-free cheese
1   small red onion, thinly sliced
1   10-oz. pkg. frozen green peas
½   bell pepper, sliced
1   c. fat-free Italian dressing

If possible, use a clear glass 2-quart straight-sided bowl in which to layer salad.

Start with a layer of half the cottage cheese, then add half the lettuce, all the black-eyed peas, all the cheese and onion, remaining lettuce, all the green peas, remaining cottage cheese, and all the bell pepper. Pour dressing over top; chill and serve.

Recipe makes 8 servings.

Grams of Fat Per Serving	Calories Per Serving
Less than 1 gram	168

SEAFOOD RICE SALAD

Light and refreshing

Dressing:

⅔ c. (6½ oz.) Kraft fat-free cream cheese
¼ c. fat-free mayonnaise
1 clove garlic, pressed
1 T. lemon juice
¼ t. seasoned salt

Salad:

4 c. cooked rice
1 c. imitation lobster meat, cut into small pieces
1 14-oz. can artichoke hearts in water, drained and
   quartered
1 16-oz. can whole-kernel corn, drained
3 green onions, chopped
½ small green pepper, chopped
2 T. chopped pimientos
½ t. dill weed
   black pepper to taste

Combine dressing ingredients in food processor or blender. Blend until smooth and set aside.

In large bowl, combine salad ingredients and toss. Add dressing and toss. Chill 1 hour before serving.

Recipe makes 6 servings.

Grams of Fat Per Serving	Calories Per Serving
1	291

Fat Free

FESTIVE TACO CORN
Tasty Mexican flair

1   16-oz. pkg. frozen corn
2   fresh green chilies, chopped
1   T. Molly McButter
1   t. dry taco seasoning
2   t. dry onion flakes
½   c. water

In medium saucepan, combine all ingredients. Simmer over low heat until corn is done and most of the water has cooked away.

Recipe makes 8 servings.

Grams of Fat Per Serving	Calories Per Serving
0	52

SPAGHETTI SALAD II
Delicious

Salad:

1 12-oz. pkg. spaghetti
1 c. fresh broccoli, chopped
1 c. frozen peas
1 medium onion, chopped
1 green pepper, chopped
1 fresh tomato, chopped
1 carrot, grated
1 T. chopped pimientos
½ c. fat-free cheese, grated

Dressing:

1 4.3-oz. pkg. Lipton onion soup mix, dry
½ c. 99% fat-free tomato soup
1 c. fat-free Italian dressing

Break spaghetti into 3"–4" pieces; cook according to package directions, drain, and rinse. In large bowl, combine all salad ingredients and toss.

Combine dressing ingredients and pour a portion over spaghetti mixture and chill. Add additional dressing just before serving.

Recipe makes 8 servings.

Grams of Fat Per Serving	Calories Per Serving
Less than 1 gram	125

Ultra Lowfat

WILTED LETTUCE SALAD

⅓ c. evaporated skim milk
1 t. dry mustard
¼ t. black pepper
5–6 c. leaf lettuce
1 green onion, chopped
4 slices turkey bacon
6 T. vinegar
2 t. sugar

Mix together evaporated milk, mustard, and black pepper and pour over combined lettuce and onion. Toss and chill.

In skillet sprayed with nonstick cooking spray, brown bacon. Cool and crumble. Add vinegar and sugar to skillet and bring almost to boil. Pour over lettuce. Top with crumbled bacon and serve warm.

Recipe makes 4 servings.

Grams of Fat Per Serving	Calories Per Serving
2	73

Ultra Lowfat

OVEN-FRIED OKRA

1 24-oz. pkg. frozen breaded okra*
  Buttermist or other butter-flavored nonstick
    cooking spray
  salt and black pepper to taste

Preheat Oven: 375°

Spray baking sheet with Buttermist and spread okra
over entire sheet; spray lightly and season with salt
and black pepper. Bake at 375° for 45–50 minutes or
until golden brown.

*Use only frozen breaded okra that has not been pre-
fried.

Recipe makes 6 servings.

Grams of Fat Per Serving	Calories Per Serving
1.5	103

Fat Free 2

MAIN DISHES
&
CASSEROLES

Ultra Lowfat

BISCUITS AND SAUSAGE GRAVY
Great country breakfast

Biscuits:

Use refrigerated canned biscuits that are either fat-free or 1 gram fat per biscuit; or make your own with Pioneer Low-Fat Biscuit Mix or a lite biscuit mix. My favorite, of course, is the Pioneer Low-Fat Biscuit Mix because of the excellent quality and taste. Prepare according to package directions.

Gravy:

1   oz. ground turkey sausage
4   T. flour
1   c. chicken broth, defatted
½   c. evaporated skim milk
1   c. skim milk
2   t. Molly McButter
    salt and black pepper to taste

In large skillet sprayed with nonstick cooking spray, brown turkey sausage. Add flour and lightly brown. In medium bowl, combine remaining ingredients. Stir with whisk and add to sausage mixture and stir until gravy thickens. Serve over hot biscuits.

Recipe makes 6 servings. Nutritional information based on gravy only.

Grams of Fat Per Serving	Calories Per Serving
1.5	71

Ultra Lowfat

CAJUN BEAN SOUP

3   c. dry mixed beans (pinto, navy, lima, black-eyed
      peas, lentils, split peas, kidney, garbanzo, etc.)
½   lb. turkey sausage
1   c. onion, chopped
1   clove garlic, minced
1   16-oz. can tomatoes, undrained
1   T. lemon juice
1–3 T. Cajun seasoning

Wash beans; place in 3½-quart crockpot; cover with water and soak overnight. Rinse and cover with 6–8 cups fresh water. Cook until beans are tender (6–8 hours on low setting plus 2 hours on high setting).

Brown turkey sausage in skillet, pouring off grease as it accumulates. Place in colander; rinse with hot water and add to beans.

Wipe out skillet and spray with nonstick cooking spray. Sauté onion and garlic until onion is clear; add to beans. Add tomatoes, lemon juice, and Cajun seasoning. NOTE: Some of the bean juice may need to be removed from crockpot to make room for the tomatoes. Cook 30 minutes on high setting.

Recipe makes 14 servings, 1 cup each.

Grams of Fat Per Serving	Calories Per Serving
2.5	163

Recipe Contributed by: Janet Potts, R.D., L.D.
Fitness/Wellness Dietitian
St. John Medical Center
Tulsa, Oklahoma

Ultra Lowfat

CHILI

1   lb. 96% fat-free ground beef
2   c. onion, chopped
1   green pepper, coarsely chopped
3   cloves garlic, pressed
3   T. chili powder
2   t. ground cumin
½   t. dried oregano leaves
1   t. salt (optional)
3   15-oz. cans red kidney beans, undrained
1   12-oz. can whole-kernel corn, undrained
2   15-oz. cans sliced tomatoes, undrained
1   8-oz. can tomato sauce

Brown ground beef in Dutch oven; drain. Add onion, green pepper, garlic, chili powder, cumin, oregano, and salt; mix well. Cook, stirring, until onion and pepper are tender.

Add beans, corn, tomatoes, and tomato sauce; stir to mix well, breaking up tomatoes with fork. Cover and simmer gently, stirring occasionally, until thickened and flavors are well blended (about 30 minutes)

Variation: May be served on baked potato or over pasta.

Recipe makes 13 servings, 1 cup each.

Grams of Fat Per Serving	Calories Per Serving
2	210

Recipe Contributed by: Janet Potts, R.D., L.D.
Fitness/Wellness Dietitian
St. John Medical Center
Tulsa, Oklahoma

Fat Free

"BIRDIES" BARLEY

1 c. barley
1 medium onion, chopped
2 stalks celery, chopped
1 10½-oz. can consommé
1 soup can water
   salt and black pepper to taste

Preheat Oven: 350°

Brown barley in skillet sprayed with nonstick cooking spray and pour into casserole. Brown onion and celery and add to barley. Add consommé, water, salt, and pepper. Cover and bake at 350° for approximately 1 hour or until all liquid has been absorbed.

Recipe makes 6 servings.

Grams of Fat Per Serving
0

Calories Per Serving
137

SEAFOOD FETTUCCINI

2   T. chopped fresh garlic
¼ c. white cooking wine
½ c. fat-free plain yogurt
½ c. fat-free sour cream
¼ c. non-fat milk
½ c. fat-free Parmesan cheese
1   t. nutmeg
1   6-oz. can medium deveined shrimp
1   6-oz. can white crab meat
1   12-oz. pkg. fettuccini pasta
    salt and black pepper to taste

Sauté garlic in wine on low heat 1–2 minutes. Add yogurt, sour cream, skim milk, Parmesan, and nutmeg. Bring to boil; reduce heat and simmer. Add shrimp and crab meat; stir until well blended and let simmer 10–15 minutes.

Cook pasta according to package directions. Add to sauce and stir well. Season with salt and pepper. Serve immediately. Garnish with parsley and slice of lemon.

Recipe makes 4 servings.

Grams of Fat Per Serving	Calories Per Serving
4	435

Recipe Contributed by: Jana R. Love, M.S.
Manager, Therapeutic Exercise Services
St. John Medical Center
Tulsa, Oklahoma

Ultra Lowfat

VEGETARIAN LASAGNE
Very good

10 lasagne noodles, cooked and drained
1 large onion, chopped
1 bell pepper, sliced (red is pretty)
2 c. (½ lb.) fresh mushrooms, sliced
1 zucchini, sliced
1 c. carrots, sliced
1 26-oz. jar Healthy Choice spaghetti sauce
1 14½-oz. can diced tomatoes
1 t. basil
1 t. garlic powder
1 t. oregano
1 t. marjoram
1 t. seasoned salt
⅓ c. fat-free liquid egg product
1 24-oz. carton fat-free cottage cheese
1 6-oz. pkg. (1½ c.) fat-free mozzarella cheese, grated
½ c. fat-free Parmesan cheese

Preheat Oven: 350°

Prepare lasagne noodles according to package directions.

Brown all vegetables in large skillet sprayed with non-stick cooking spray and simmer until almost tender (about 10 minutes).

In large bowl, combine and stir spaghetti sauce, tomatoes, and spices. In medium bowl, stir together egg product and cottage cheese.

In 9" × 13" glass baking dish sprayed with nonstick cooking spray, layer the noodles, half the cooked vegetables, half the cottage cheese mixture, half the tomato mixture, and half the mozzarella cheese. Repeat layers, ending with remaining mozzarella cheese, and top with Parmesan. Cover and bake at 350° for 1 hour.

Recipe makes 8 servings.

Grams of Fat Per Serving	Calories Per Serving
3	358

Ultra Lowfat

STUFFED POTATO SKINS
Delicious—a meal in one

5 medium baking potatoes
1 lb. boneless, skinless chicken breasts, cut into
     small pieces
1 c. (¼ lb.) fresh mushrooms, sliced
1 small onion, chopped
½ green pepper, chopped
1 10-oz. can Campbell's 97% fat-free cream of
     mushroom soup
½ c. fat-free sour cream
¼ t. garlic powder
   salt and black pepper to taste
   paprika

Preheat Oven: 425°

Bake potatoes at 425° about 1 hour or until done. Cool on rack until cool enough to handle. Slice each in half lengthwise and remove some potato from center. Leave enough around edges so potato will keep its shape.

Brown chicken pieces in skillet sprayed with nonstick cooking spray. Add mushrooms, onion, and green pepper and brown. Drain off any excess liquid. Add mushroom soup, sour cream, garlic powder, salt, and pepper. Stir until mixed thoroughly. Spoon into potato halves.

Place stuffed potatoes on baking sheet sprayed with nonstick cooking spray and sprinkle paprika on top. Bake at 350° for 25–30 minutes.

Save potato centers to mash or make potato cubes for another meal.

Recipe makes 5 servings.

Grams of Fat Per Serving	Calories Per Serving
4	464

SHRIMP CREOLE

2½ c. onion, finely chopped
1¾ c. celery, finely chopped
1½ c. bell pepper, finely chopped
2   t. garlic, minced
1   bay leaf
2   t. salt
1   t. white pepper
½   t. black pepper
½   t. cayenne pepper
2½ c. shrimp stock (Knorr instant fish bouillon)
1   t. Tabasco sauce
1   t. thyme
2   t. basil
3   c. diced tomatoes
1½ c. tomato sauce
2   t. sugar
3   lbs. large shrimp, peeled
5   c. rice, cooked

Add onion, celery, and bell pepper to large saucepan sprayed with Buttermist. Cook over medium-high heat until onions begin to brown. Add garlic, bay leaf, salt, white pepper, black pepper, cayenne pepper, shrimp stock, Tabasco, thyme, and basil. Cook over medium heat 15 minutes.

Add tomatoes; turn heat to low and stir occasionally. Add tomato sauce and sugar. Simmer 30 minutes, uncovered, stirring occasionally. Turn heat off and add shrimp; stir 5 minutes or until shrimp are pink. Remove bay leaf. Serve immediately over hot rice.

Recipe makes 8 servings.

Grams of Fat Per Serving	Calories Per Serving
2.5	347

Recipe Contributed by: Susan Loberg
Cooking Now
Jonesboro, Arkansas

Ultra Lowfat

STUFFED PEPPERS

½   lb. 96% fat-free ground beef
1   14½-oz. can Italian-style tomatoes
½   c. water
1   t. Italian seasoning
½   t. salt (optional)
1½ c. instant rice, uncooked
4   large bell peppers

Preheat Oven: 350°

Brown ground beef in large skillet; pour off grease, if any. Add tomatoes, water, Italian seasoning, and salt. Bring to boil. Stir in instant rice. Cover; remove from heat and let stand 5 minutes or until rice has absorbed liquid.

Cut each pepper in half lengthwise and remove stem and seeds. Place in baking dish and fill with rice mixture. Bake at 350° for 30 minutes or until peppers are tender-crisp.

Variation: Omit baking and store unbaked stuffed peppers in refrigerator until ready for use. Microwave individual peppers on high for 2 minutes.

Recipe makes 4 servings.

Grams of Fat Per Serving	Calories Per Serving
2.8	239

Recipe Contributed by: Janet Potts, R.D., L.D.
Fitness/Wellness Dietitian
St. John Medical Center
Tulsa, Oklahoma

Ultra Lowfat

HUNGARIAN CHICKEN GOULASH
Grandma Merle's Old World recipe

3 large onions, coarsely chopped (about 3 cups)
2 T. paprika
2 skinless chicken breasts (leave in bone)
1 t. salt
2 potatoes, peeled and quartered
  water

Sauté onions until brown in Dutch oven lightly sprayed with nonstick cooking spray. Remove from heat; cool, add paprika and mix well. Return to heat and add chicken, turning so all pieces are coated with onion mixture. Sprinkle with salt; cover and simmer 1 hour, stirring occasionally and adding water if necessary. Add potatoes and 1½ cups water. Cook 45 minutes, adding more water if necessary. Serve with dumplings or rice.

Recipe makes 4 servings.

Grams of Fat Per Serving	Calories Per Serving
3	242

Original Recipe: Old family recipe by Rose Merle with modifications by Linda Merle, R.N. II
Healthy LifeStyle Programs System Manager
St. John Medical Center
Tulsa, Oklahoma

SAUSAGE AND RICE CASSEROLE
Very good

1   12-oz. roll ground turkey sausage
1   green pepper, chopped
6   green onions, chopped
1   bunch celery, chopped
    salt and black pepper to taste
2   3-oz. pkgs. dry chicken noodle soup (Ramen lowfat
    noodles)
4½ c. boiling water
1   c. brown rice, uncooked
1   8-oz. can water chestnuts, drained
1   c. fat-free sour cream

Preheat Oven: 350°

Brown turkey sausage; drain and rinse with hot water, then return to skillet. Add green pepper, onions, and celery and sauté 5–10 minutes. Add salt and black pepper.

Break up noodles for soup and cook in boiling water 2 minutes. Add rice and water chestnuts and stir. Discard flavor packet.

Combine all ingredients and stir. Pour into large casserole sprayed with nonstick cooking spray; cover and bake at 350° for 1½–2 hours.

Recipe makes 10 servings.

Grams of Fat Per Serving	Calories Per Serving
5	217

ERMA'S CHICKEN
WITH CURRY SAUCE

4   boneless, skinless chicken breasts, cut into small
    pieces
1   small onion, finely chopped
2   cloves garlic, pressed
½   t. garlic salt
¼   c. celery, finely chopped
1   medium apple, peeled and finely chopped
1   banana, diced
2   T. curry powder
1   c. chicken broth, defatted
½   c. stewed diced tomatoes
2   t. Molly McButter
½   c. golden raisins
4   c. rice, cooked

In large skillet sprayed with nonstick cooking spray, brown chicken pieces and onion. Add garlic and garlic salt and continue to brown. Add celery, apple, banana, and curry powder. Cook 1 minute. Add chicken broth, tomatoes, and Molly McButter. Stir and simmer over low heat 15 minutes. Add raisins last 5 minutes of cooking. Serve warm over rice.

Recipe makes 6 servings.

Grams of Fat Per Serving	Calories Per Serving
3	338

Recipe Contributed by: Erma Brown

Ultra Lowfat

BEEF AND NOODLE CASSEROLE

1   8-oz. pkg. medium lowfat (1 g fat) noodles
1   c. fat-free cottage cheese
1   8-oz. carton fat-free sour cream
½   c. onion, chopped
½   c. green pepper, chopped
1   lb. lowfat ground beef
1   12-oz. can tomato paste
1   4-oz. can sliced mushrooms, undrained
1   t. garlic powder
    black pepper to taste
1   c. fat-free cheddar or American cheese, shredded

Preheat Oven: 350°

Cook noodles according to package directions and drain well. Mix gently with cottage cheese, sour cream, onion, and green pepper.

Brown ground beef in skillet, stirring to crumble, and drain. Add tomato paste, mushrooms with liquid, garlic powder, and black pepper. Mix well and simmer 5 minutes, stirring occasionally.

Spoon half the noodle mixture into 9" × 13" baking dish sprayed with nonstick cooking spray; top with half the meat mixture, then repeat noodle layer and meat layer. Sprinkle evenly with shredded cheese. Bake at 350° for 30 minutes or until cheese is melted and casserole is thoroughly heated.

Recipe makes 8 servings.

Grams of Fat Per Serving	Calories Per Serving
2.5	267

Recipe Contributed by: Marilyn Stutsman, R.N.
Therapeutic Exercise Services
St. John Medical Center
Tulsa, Oklahoma

Ultra Lowfat

CHICKEN-FRIED CHICKEN WITH CREAM GRAVY

One of my very best—don't miss this one

Chicken:

4 boneless, skinless chicken breasts
2 egg whites, slightly beaten
2 c. corn flakes, crushed
   salt and black pepper to taste

Gravy:

4 T. flour
1 c. chicken broth, defatted
½ c. evaporated skim milk
1 c. skim milk
2 t. Molly McButter
   salt and black pepper to taste

Lightly pound chicken breasts with table knife handle until they are thinner, larger, and lightly tenderized. Dip in egg white and roll in crushed corn flakes. In skillet sprayed with nonstick cooking spray, brown and cook over medium-low heat 5–6 minutes on each side (will burn easily; keep heat fairly low). Turn only once. When chicken is done, remove from skillet.

Add flour to skillet and brown over medium heat, stir-ring occasionally. This will burn easily. Remove skillet from heat and set aside.

In medium bowl, combine remaining gravy ingredients. Using a whisk, with skillet still removed from heat, add gravy liquid while stirring. Return to heat, whisk and stir until gravy thickens. Serve gravy spooned over chicken. Enjoy! You'll think you've died and gone to heaven!

Recipe makes 4 servings.

Grams of Fat Per Serving	Calories Per Serving
4	314

Ultra Lowfat

LITE REUBEN SANDWICH
Wonderful

1   medium onion, sliced
4   slices rye bread
    spicy hot mustard
½   lb. lite ham, shaved
1   16-oz. can sauerkraut, well drained
4   slices fat-free Swiss cheese

In large skillet sprayed with nonstick cooking spray, brown and sauté onions.

Spread bread slices with mustard and place on cooking sheet sprayed with nonstick cooking spray. Place shaved ham on each bread slice, then spoon on sauerkraut. Top with 1 slice cheese and spoon on onions. Place under broiler to melt cheese. Serve warm.

Recipe makes 4 servings.

Grams of Fat Per Serving	Calories Per Serving
4.5	222

Ultra Lowfat

BROCCOLI AND RICE CASSEROLE

1   10¾-oz. can Campbell's 99% fat-free cream of
      chicken soup
2   t. dry onion flakes
2   t. Molly McButter
½   c. fat-free sour cream
1   2-oz. pkg. dry ranch dressing mix
1   14-oz. can chicken broth, defatted
2   c. uncooked Minute Rice
1½ c. fresh broccoli, chopped or 1 10-oz. box frozen
      broccoli
½   c. fat-free cheese, grated
      black pepper to taste

Preheat Oven: 350°

In large bowl, combine soup, onion flakes, Molly
McButter, sour cream, dry dressing mix, and chicken
broth. Beat with electric mixer until smooth. Add rice,
broccoli, and cheese and stir with spoon. Add black
pepper. Pour into casserole sprayed with nonstick
cooking spray; cover and bake at 350° for 40 minutes.

Recipe makes 8 servings.

Grams of Fat Per Serving	Calories Per Serving
1	139

Fat Free

GREEN CHILE RICE

1   10-oz. can green chile enchilada sauce
1   4-oz. can chopped green chilies
1   T. dry onion flakes
2   t. Molly McButter
1   t. garlic salt
1   14-oz. can chicken broth, defatted
2   c. uncooked Minute Rice
½   c. fat-free cheese, shredded
    black pepper to taste

Preheat Oven: 350°

In large bowl, combine enchilada sauce, green chilies, onion flakes, Molly McButter, garlic salt, and chicken broth. Add rice and shredded cheese and stir. Add black pepper. Pour into casserole sprayed with non-stick cooking spray and bake uncovered at 350° for 40 minutes.

Recipe makes 8 servings.

Grams of Fat Per Serving	Calories Per Serving
0	79

Ultra Lowfat

TABASCO CHICKEN
Hot and spicy

4 boneless, skinless chicken breasts
   Tabasco sauce
   garlic salt
   onion powder
   black pepper

Rinse and pat dry chicken breasts. Generously shake Tabasco sauce on each side, then season each side with garlic salt, onion powder, and black pepper.

Brown and simmer in skillet sprayed with nonstick cooking spray until done and tender. Serve.

Recipe makes 4 servings.

Grams of Fat Per Serving	Calories Per Serving
4	197

Ultra Lowfat

FRENCH ONION CHICKEN AND POTATO BAKE

Easy and tastes delicious

4 boneless, skinless chicken breasts
   garlic powder
   black pepper
2 potatoes, peeled and cut into chunks
1 10½-oz. can Campbell's French onion soup

Preheat Oven: 350°

Season both sides of chicken breasts with garlic powder and black pepper. Brown in skillet sprayed with nonstick cooking spray and place in 8" baking dish sprayed with nonstick cooking spray.

Cover chicken with potato chunks. Pour soup over top and sprinkle with black pepper. Cover and bake at 350° for 40–50 minutes or until potatoes are done.

Recipe makes 4 servings.

Grams of Fat Per Serving	Calories Per Serving
6	303

Ultra Lowfat

BARBECUE CHICKEN AND COLESLAW SANDWICH

Don't knock it until you try it—it's wonderful

1 lb. boneless, skinless chicken breasts
1 c. barbecue sauce
2 t. dry onion flakes
⅓ c. buttermilk coleslaw for each sandwich
   (see page 55)
6 lite hamburger buns

Brown chicken in skillet sprayed with nonstick cooking spray. Cover and simmer until tender. Remove from skillet and cool until easily handled.

Cut chicken in about 2" pieces and shred with fingers or chop into small pieces. Return to skillet and cover with barbecue sauce. Add onion flakes and stir and simmer over low heat.

Place few spoonfuls of meat on each hamburger bun and top with scoop of coleslaw. Place top of bun on sandwich and enjoy.

Recipe makes 6 servings. (Figures do not include coleslaw.)

Grams of Fat Per Serving	Calories Per Serving
4	213

Ultra Lowfat

SWEET AND SOUR CHICKEN ROLLS

Easy and delicious

12 egg roll wrappers

Filling:

1   lb. boneless, skinless chicken breasts, cut into
      small pieces
½   t. garlic salt
1   15¼-oz. can pineapple tidbits (save juice)
2   t. lite soy sauce
½   large green pepper, chopped
1   medium white onion, chopped
⅓   c. La Choy sweet and sour sauce (save remaining
      sauce in jar for dipping)

Preheat Oven: 350°

Add chicken pieces to skillet sprayed with nonstick cooking spray and start to brown. As chicken is browning, add garlic salt and continue cooking until golden brown. Add juice from pineapple and soy sauce and stir and simmer over medium heat until all liquid is absorbed. Set aside to cool.

In large bowl, combine all remaining ingredients and toss. Add chicken and mix.

Place about ¼ cup chicken mixture in center of each egg roll wrapper. Fold and roll wrapper around filling according to package directions.

Place finished rolls on baking sheet sprayed with nonstick cooking spray, then spray tops lightly with nonstick spray. Bake at 350° for 25–30 minutes or until golden brown. Serve warm with sweet and sour sauce.

Recipe makes 12 rolls. Serving size is 2 rolls.

Grams of Fat Per Serving	Calories Per Serving
2.5	245

PIMIENTO CHICKEN
This is very good

4   boneless, skinless chicken breasts
½ t. garlic salt
    black pepper to taste
1   c. (8-oz.) Kraft fat-free cream cheese
1   4-oz. jar chopped pimientos
2   t. dry onion flakes
¼ c. chicken broth, defatted
½ green pepper, chopped

Preheat Oven: 350°

Brown chicken breasts in skillet sprayed with nonstick cooking spray. Season while cooking with garlic salt and black pepper.

In medium bowl, combine cream cheese, pimientos, onion flakes, chicken broth, and green pepper. Stir until well blended.

Place chicken breasts in casserole sprayed with non-stick cooking spray. Pour cream cheese mixture over top and bake at 350° for 35 minutes.

Recipe makes 4 servings.

Grams of Fat Per Serving	Calories Per Serving
4	257

HONEY DIJON OVEN CHICKEN
Wonderful flavor

½ c. honey
¼ c. Dijon mustard
1 clove garlic, pressed
1 small onion, finely chopped
4 boneless, skinless chicken breasts
2 c. crushed corn flakes
  salt and black pepper to taste

Preheat Oven: 350°

In small bowl, combine honey, mustard, garlic, and onion.

Dip chicken breasts in mixture and roll in corn flakes. Place on baking sheet sprayed with nonstick cooking spray and sprinkle with salt and pepper. Discard any remaining honey mustard mixture when finished.

Bake at 350° for 30–35 minutes.

Recipe makes 4 servings.

Grams of Fat Per Serving	Calories Per Serving
4	397

Ultra Lowfat

SAVORY APRICOT CHICKEN
Delicious over rice or pasta

4   boneless, skinless chicken breasts
½ pkg. Lipton golden onion soup mix, dry
½ pkg. Lipton savory herb and garlic soup mix, dry
1   12-oz. jar apricot preserves
½ c. chicken broth, defatted

Preheat Oven: 350°

Place chicken breasts in baking dish sprayed with non-stick cooking spray. Combine remaining ingredients and mix well. Pour over chicken and bake uncovered at 350° for 45–50 minutes.

Recipe makes 4 servings.

Grams of Fat Per Serving	Calories Per Serving
4	491

Ultra Lowfat

JALAPEÑO CHICKEN
Spicy, but not too hot

1 lb. boneless, skinless chicken breasts
½ t. Molly McButter
1 8- or 10-oz. jar jalapeño jelly
⅓ c. chicken broth, defatted
1 4.3-oz. pkg. Lipton onion soup mix, dry
4 c. rice, cooked

Preheat Oven: 350°

Place chicken breasts in 8" baking dish sprayed with nonstick cooking spray and sprinkle with Molly McButter.

In medium bowl, combine and stir together jalapeño jelly, chicken broth, and onion soup mix. Pour over chicken and bake at 350° for 45 minutes. Serve over rice.

Recipe makes 4 servings.

Grams of Fat Per Serving	Calories Per Serving
4	597

Ultra Lowfat

NOODLE CASSEROLE
Wonderful

1 12-oz. pkg. No Yolk noodles
½ t. Molly McButter
1 lb. ground turkey breast or chicken breast
1 small onion, chopped
1 6-oz. can tomato paste
⅓ c. chicken broth, defatted
¼ t. garlic powder
½ t. Worcestershire sauce
salt and black pepper to taste
1½ c. fat-free cottage cheese
1 c. (8-oz.) Kraft fat-free cream cheese
⅓ c. fat-free sour cream

Cook noodles according to package directions; rinse, drain, and sprinkle with Molly McButter.

Brown meat and onion in skillet sprayed with nonstick cooking spray. Add tomato paste, chicken broth, garlic powder, Worcestershire sauce, salt, and black pepper. Remove from heat and set aside to cool.

In large bowl, combine cottage cheese, cream cheese, and sour cream. Stir with spoon until well blended. Add meat mixture and stir. Fold in noodles. Pour mixture into large casserole sprayed with nonstick cooking spray; cover and bake at 350° for 35–40 minutes.

Recipe makes 8 servings.

Grams of Fat Per Serving	Calories Per Serving
3	326

Ultra Lowfat

CLAM LINGUINE
For seafood lovers

½   c. evaporated skim milk
1½ c. skim milk
2   6-oz. cans minced clams with liquid
½   small onion, chopped
1   clove garlic, pressed
¼   c. fat-free sour cream
¼   c. fat-free Parmesan cheese
2   t. Molly McButter
½   t. parsley
    salt and black pepper to taste
1   T. cornstarch (optional)
4   c. cooked linguine noodles

In large saucepan, combine all ingredients except cornstarch and noodles. Simmer and stir over medium-low heat 5–10 minutes. Use cornstarch to thicken if desired.

Serve over noodles.

Recipe makes 4 servings.

Grams of Fat Per Serving	Calories Per Serving
1.5	319

Ultra Lowfat

ONION-MUSHROOM MEAT LOAF
Makes great sandwiches

2   lbs. ground turkey breast or chicken breast
1   4.3-oz. pkg. dry Lipton onion-mushroom soup mix
2   egg whites, slightly beaten
½   c. fat-free sour cream
¼   t. black pepper
¼   t. garlic powder

Preheat Oven: 350°

In large bowl, combine all ingredients until well mixed.
Pour into loaf pan or dish sprayed with nonstick cooking spray and bake at 350° for 1 hour and 20 minutes.
Remove and serve. Wonderful served with baked
potato.

Recipe makes 8 servings.

Grams of Fat Per Serving	Calories Per Serving
4	235

Ultra Lowfat

ITALIAN PASTA SOUP

Try on a cold winter night with garlic toast

1   lb. ground turkey breast or chicken breast
1   16-oz. can stewed tomatoes
1   15-oz. can kidney beans, drained and rinsed
½   c. canned or fresh julienne carrots
1   14-oz. can Swanson beef broth, defatted
1   8-oz. can tomato sauce
1   stalk celery, chopped
2   t. dry onion flakes
1   clove garlic, pressed
1   c. uncooked pasta
1   1⅓-oz. pkg. dry spaghetti sauce mix
1   2-oz. pkg. dry ranch dressing mix
    salt and black pepper to taste
    dash of seasoned salt
3   c. water

Brown meat in large pot sprayed with nonstick cooking spray. Add remaining ingredients and simmer only long enough to cook pasta. DO NOT OVERCOOK. Serve warm with garlic toast.

Recipe makes 6 servings.

Grams of Fat Per Serving	Calories Per Serving
2	419

Ultra Lowfat

ONION CHEESE PIE

One of my favorites

2 large fat-free flour tortillas
   Buttermist nonstick cooking spray
1 t. Molly McButter
1 16-oz. carton fat-free cottage cheese
⅓ c. fat-free liquid egg product
2 t. dry onion flakes
1 medium onion, thinly sliced
⅓ cup fat-free Parmesan cheese
5 slices fat-free Swiss cheese
⅓ c. fat-free cheddar cheese, grated
1 large ripe tomato, thinly sliced
   garlic salt
   black pepper to taste

Preheat Oven: 325°

Place 1 tortilla in large pie plate sprayed with nonstick cooking spray. Spray tortilla lightly with Buttermist and sprinkle with ½ t. Molly McButter. Repeat process with second tortilla on top of the other.

In large bowl, combine cottage cheese, egg product, and onion flakes and mix with spoon. Pour half over tortillas and gently smooth and spread with spoon.

Add layers in this order: half of the sliced onion, all the Parmesan and Swiss cheese, remaining cottage cheese mixture, all the cheddar cheese, remaining sliced onion, and all the sliced tomato. Sprinkle top with garlic salt and black pepper.

Bake at 325° for 1 hour and 20 minutes. Cool slightly before slicing.

Recipe makes 8 servings.

Grams of Fat Per Serving	Calories Per Serving
1	128

Ultra Lowfat

PARMESAN NOODLES

Very tasty complement to any meal

1   12-oz. pkg. No Yolk noodles
1   T. plus 2 t. Molly McButter added to water to boil
       noodles
     butter-flavored nonstick cooking spray
¼ c. fat-free Parmesan cheese
     black pepper to taste

Prepare noodles according to package directions. I like
to use about 1 tablespoon Molly McButter in water
when boiling noodles. Drain and rinse noodles, drain-
ing only slightly to leave some moisture to help melt
and dissolved cheese and Molly McButter.

Spray noodles lightly with nonstick cooking spray
and toss. Sprinkle with 2 teaspoons Molly McButter
and Parmesan and toss. Add black pepper to taste and
toss. Serve immediately.

Recipe makes 4 servings.

Grams of Fat Per Serving	Calories Per Serving
1	327

Ultra Lowfat

OVEN CRISPY
ONION-MUSHROOM CHICKEN
Yummy!

¾ c. Kraft fat-free mayonnaise
1 T. dry Lipton onion-mushroom soup mix
4 boneless, skinless chicken breasts
3–4 c. corn flakes, crushed
 salt and black pepper to taste

Preheat Oven: 350°

Combine mayonnaise and dry soup mix; let stand 5–10 minutes so onion flakes will soften.

If chicken breasts are wet, pat dry. Dip chicken breasts in mayonnaise mixture and roll in corn flake crumbs and place in pan or cookie sheet sprayed with nonstick cooking spray. Season each with salt and pepper. Bake at 350° for 30–35 minutes.

Recipe makes 4 servings.

Grams of Fat Per Serving	Calories Per Serving
4	317

Ultra Lowfat

SWEET AND SOUR CHICKEN SALAD
Refreshing

1   lb. boneless, skinless chicken breasts, cut into
    small pieces
½ t. garlic salt
1   15¼-oz. can pineapple tidbits (save juice)
2   t. lite soy sauce
½ large green pepper, chopped
1   medium white onion, chopped
¼ c. carrot, grated
½ c. La Choy sweet and sour sauce

Brown chicken pieces in skillet sprayed with nonstick
cooking spray. Add garlic salt and continue cooking
until chicken is golden brown. Add juice from pineapple
and soy sauce; simmer and stir over medium-low heat
until all juice is absorbed. Set aside to cool.

In large bowl, combine vegetables and pineapple and
toss. Add cooled chicken and mix. Pour on sweet and
sour sauce and toss. Serve on large lettuce leaf.

Recipe makes 6 servings

Grams of Fat Per Serving	Calories Per Serving
3	212

Ultra Lowfat

TACO CHICKEN SALAD

1 lb. boneless, skinless chicken breasts, cut into
   small pieces
1 1¼-oz. pkg. taco seasoning
½ c. taco sauce
2 t. dry onion flakes
1 c. canned whole-kernel corn, drained
¼ c. green chilies, chopped
½ c. fat-free sour cream
1 t. dry ranch dressing mix

Add chicken pieces to skillet sprayed with nonstick cooking spray. Sprinkle with taco seasoning and stir over
medium heat. Add taco sauce and onion flakes and stir.
Reduce heat to low and simmer until all liquid is cooked
into meat. Remove from heat and chill slightly.

Combine seasoned chicken with all remaining ingredients in medium-size bowl. Stir until thoroughly mixed
and chill for a few hours before serving.

Serve on bun or bagel as sandwich. Can be rolled in
flour or corn tortilla or served on lettuce leaf and garnished
with chopped tomatoes and grated fat-free cheese.

Recipe makes 6 servings.

Grams of Fat Per Serving	Calories Per Serving
3	217

Ultra Lowfat

HONEY CRUNCHY CHICKEN
This is spicy and sweet

¼	c. honey plus little more for garnish
½	c. Kraft fat-free mayonnaise
¼–½	t. blackened or Cajun spices (to taste)
	salt and black pepper to taste
4	boneless, skinless chicken breasts
1½	c. Grape Nuts cereal

In small bowl, mix honey, mayonnaise, and spices. Pour into container large enough to dip chicken breasts. Use another container large enough to roll dipped chicken in Grape Nuts.

Dip chicken breasts in honey mixture, then roll in Grape Nuts until covered. Place in skillet sprayed with non-stick cooking spray on medium-low heat. Drizzle about 1 teaspoon honey over each chicken breast.

Cover and simmer 15 minutes. Turn and cook additional 15 minutes. Drizzle honey on again after turning. Try not to turn more than once, as this disturbs coating. Be sure chicken is covered with lid during cooking.

Recipe makes 4 servings.

Grams of Fat Per Serving	Calories Per Serving
4	380

Ultra Lowfat

CRISPY HONEY DIJON CHICKEN
Slightly sweet and delicious

¾ c. Kraft fat-free mayonnaise
1 T. dry Hidden Valley Honey Dijon Salad Dressing
mix
4 boneless, skinless chicken breasts
¾ c. Kellogg's Apple Raisin Crisp cereal, crushed
salt and black pepper to taste
1 12-oz. pkg. No Yolk noodles (optional)

Preheat Oven: 350°

Mix together mayonnaise and dry salad dressing mix. If there is any moisture on chicken breasts, pat dry. Dip chicken in mayonnaise mixture and roll in crushed cereal.

Place on cookie sheet or pan sprayed with nonstick cooking spray. Season with salt and pepper. Bake at 350° for 30–35 minutes.

Optional: While chicken is baking, prepare noodles according to package directions. Serve chicken breasts on bed of noodles.

Recipe makes 4 servings.

Grams of Fat Per Serving	Calories Per Serving
5	557

CREOLE GRAVY CHICKEN WITH RICE

Very good and different—one of my favorites

Chicken:

4	boneless, skinless chicken breasts
	garlic powder to taste
	black pepper to taste
1	4.3-oz. pkg. Lipton rice and sauce mix, mushroom flavor
2	c. chicken broth, defatted
2	t. Molly McButter

Creole Gravy:

¼	c. chicken broth, defatted
⅛	c. evaporated skim milk
½	c. fat-free sour cream
4	T. spicy brown mustard
¼	t. blackened or Cajun spices
1½	t. sugar
1	t. Molly McButter

Preheat Oven: 350°

Season chicken breasts with garlic powder and black pepper. Brown on both sides in skillet sprayed with nonstick cooking spray.

Sprinkle rice and sauce mix evenly over bottom of 8"
or 9" square baking dish sprayed with nonstick cooking
spray. Add 2 cups chicken broth. Sprinkle 2 teaspoons
Molly McButter over top. Place chicken breasts over
mixture and bake uncovered at 350° for 30–35 minutes or until most of the juice has been absorbed
by the rice.

While chicken and rice are cooking, prepare creole
gravy. In small saucepan, combine all ingredients and
stir over low heat.

Pour creole gravy over each chicken breast just before
serving.

Recipe makes 4 servings.

Grams of Fat Per Serving	Calories Per Serving
4	437

Ultra Lowfat

CHILI DOGS IN A BLANKET
... with a deliciously different twist

6	fat-free hot dogs
6	t. prepared mustard (or to taste)
3	t. dry Lipton onion soup mix
3	t. dry ranch dressing mix
6	t. Williams Chili Makin's (in jar)
2½	c. Pioneer Low-Fat Biscuit Mix*
1	c. evaporated skim milk

Preheat Oven: 350°

Slice each hot dog down center lengthwise (*do not cut all the way through*). Squirt a strip of mustard down center of split.

Add ½ teaspoon onion soup mix and ½ teaspoon dressing mix in each split on top of mustard. Add 1 teaspoon Chili Makin's on each. Set stuffed hot dogs aside.

Combine biscuit mix and evaporated milk and mix thoroughly. Dough will be stiff.

Spray large dinner plate with nonstick cooking spray and spray your hands lightly. Using your hands, roll about ½ cup dough into ball. Use your fingers to flatten ball of dough on plate until about the size of a small tortilla. Place a stuffed hot dog across center of dough. Wrap dough around hot dog and pinch to seal. Repeat for each hot dog.

Place in 9" × 13" casserole sprayed with nonstick cooking spray, leaving space between each for dough to expand. Bake at 350° for 25 minutes or until golden brown.

Recipe makes 6 servings.

*If you can't find Pioneer Low-Fat Biscuit Mix in your area, use a light biscuit mix; however, this will add a few grams of fat to each serving.

Grams of Fat Per Serving	Calories Per Serving
2	379

CORN QUICHE

½ c. fat-free liquid egg product
¾ c. Pioneer Low-Fat Biscuit Mix*
1 c. fat-free cottage cheese
½ c. fat-free sour cream
2 t. Molly McButter
1 16-oz. can whole-kernel corn, drained
2 t. dry onion flakes
½ c. fat-free cheese, grated

Preheat Oven: 350°

Combine egg product, biscuit mix, cottage cheese, sour cream, and Molly McButter and beat with electric mixer about 2 minutes.

With spoon, fold in corn, onion flakes, and grated cheese and mix thoroughly. Pour into 10" pie plate sprayed with nonstick cooking spray and bake at 350° for 30–35 minutes.

Recipe makes 6 servings.

*If you can't find Pioneer Low-Fat Biscuit Mix in your area, use a light biscuit mix; however, this will add a few grams of fat to each serving.

Grams of Fat Per Serving	Calories Per Serving
1	232

Ultra Lowfat

CHICKEN GUMBO

1	lb. boneless, skinless chicken breasts, cut into small pieces
1	slice turkey bacon
¼–½	t. Cajun or blackened spices (more is better)
1	14½-oz. can stewed tomatoes
1	14-oz. can chicken broth, defatted
2	t. dry onion flakes
½	c. frozen, cut okra
1	stalk celery, chopped
2	T. green pepper, chopped
⅛	t. garlic powder or salt
2	c. water
¾	c. instant rice
½	2-oz. pkg. ranch dressing mix, dry
	salt and black pepper to taste
	dash of seasoned salt

In large pot sprayed with nonstick cooking spray, brown chicken pieces with turkey bacon. Season with Cajun or blackened spices while browning. Add remaining ingredients and simmer until rice is done.

Recipe makes 6 servings.

Grams of Fat Per Serving	Calories Per Serving
3.5	217

Ultra Lowfat

BREAKFAST BURRITO

½ t. dry onion flakes
½ c. fat-free liquid egg product
1 slice turkey bacon, cooked and crumbled
1 slice Kraft fat-free cheese, torn into small pieces
1 T. green chilies, chopped
   salt and black pepper to taste
   dash of Tabasco sauce (optional)
2 t. fat-free sour cream
1 small fat-free flour tortilla

Add onion flakes to egg product and set aside 5–10 minutes for onion flakes to soften.

In small bowl, combine and mix all ingredients except sour cream and tortilla. Scramble mixture in skillet sprayed with nonstick cooking spray over medium-low heat. Cheese will burn if heat is too high.

When egg mixture is almost done, stir in sour cream. Place on tortilla and roll up. Enjoy.

Recipe makes 1 serving.

Grams of Fat Per Serving	Calories Per Serving
2	243

Ultra Lowfat

CHICKEN SALAD DELUXE
Rich and creamy

½ c. (4 oz.) Kraft fat-free cream cheese
½ c. fat-free sour cream
½ t. seasoned salt (optional)
½ t. garlic salt or powder
  black pepper to taste
4 boneless, skinless chicken breasts, cooked and cut
    into small pieces
1 14-oz. can artichoke hearts, drained and quartered
1 4-oz. jar chopped pimientos
1 medium onion, chopped
½ c. celery, chopped

In small bowl, combine cream cheese, sour cream, seasoned salt, garlic salt, and black pepper and stir. In large bowl, combine remaining ingredients.

Pour cream cheese mixture over chicken and vegetable mixture and toss. Chill and serve.

Recipe makes 6 servings.

Grams of Fat Per Serving	Calories Per Serving
3	248

STUFFED BELL PEPPERS
Delicious

4   medium bell peppers
1   lb. ground chicken breast or turkey breast
½ 10-oz. can Campbell's 97% fat-free cream of
       mushroom soup
½ c. uncooked rice
2   egg whites
1   T. dry onion flakes
½ t. garlic powder
½ t. salt (optional)
½ t. black pepper

Preheat Oven: 375°

Cut tops off bell peppers and remove seeds. Set aside.

In large bowl, combine remaining ingredients and mix
well. Fill peppers with mixture and bake in baking dish
sprayed with nonstick cooking spray at 375° for
40–50 minutes.

Recipe makes 4 servings.

Grams of Fat Per Serving	Calories Per Serving
3	283

Ultra Lowfat

MEXICAN BURGERS
Delicious

1   lb. ground turkey breast or chicken breast
½ c. onion, chopped
¼ c. green chilies, chopped
1   clove garlic, pressed or ½ t. garlic powder
½ t. chili powder
½ t. Tabasco sauce
     salt and black pepper to taste

Combine all ingredients and mix thoroughly. Shape into patties and cook in large skillet sprayed with non-stick cooking spray.

Makes 4–6 burgers, depending on size and thickness desired. Serve on lite hamburger buns.

Recipe makes 6 servings.

Grams of Fat Per Serving	Calories Per Serving
2.5	91

Ultra Lowfat

TUNA LASAGNE

1   10-oz. can Campbell's 97% fat-free cream of
       mushroom soup
⅓   c. fat-free sour cream
1   c. chicken broth, defatted
2   6⅛-oz. cans water-packed tuna
2   t. dry onion flakes
1   4-oz. can sliced mushrooms, drained
       black pepper to taste
1½ c. fat-free cottage cheese
½   c. fat-free liquid egg product
1   8-oz. pkg. lasagne noodles, cooked and drained
1   c. fat-free mozzarella cheese, shredded
⅓   c. fat-free Parmesan cheese
1   t. garlic salt

Preheat Oven: 350°

In large bowl, stir together soup, sour cream, chicken broth, tuna, onion flakes, and mushrooms. Mix thoroughly. Add black pepper and mix.

In small bowl, combine cottage cheese and egg product.

In large baking dish sprayed with nonstick cooking spray, layer half *each* of the noodles, mozzarella, tuna mixture, Parmesan, cottage cheese mixture, and garlic salt. Repeat layers. Bake at 350° for 35–40 minutes.

Grams of Fat Per Serving	Calories Per Serving
2	261

Ultra Lowfat

OLD-FASHIONED HOMESTYLE NOODLES
Wonderful—don't miss this one!

2   c. water
1   14-oz. can chicken broth, defatted
1   12-oz. pkg. Reames Free frozen home-style
    noodles
1   stalk celery, chopped
1   T. dry onion flakes
1   10¾-oz. can Campbell's 97% fat-free cream of
    chicken soup
1   c. skim milk
1½ T. Molly McButter
    salt and black pepper to taste
1   10-oz. pkg. frozen peas
½   c. fat-free sour cream

Bring water and chicken broth to boil in large kettle. Add noodles, celery, and onion flakes and simmer 20 minutes.

Add remaining ingredients except peas and sour cream. Simmer 2 minutes. Add peas and sour cream; simmer 3–4 minutes. DO NOT BOIL. Serve.

Recipe makes 6 servings.

Grams of Fat Per Serving	Calories Per Serving
1.5	278

Ultra Lowfat

PHILLY TURKEY
WITH SWISS ON A BAGEL

A delicious sandwich

4–5 thin strips green pepper
½   small onion, sliced
2–4 T. fat-free Italian salad dressing
1   large plain bagel, cut in half
3   oz. shaved turkey luncheon meat
1   slice Bordens fat-free Swiss cheese

Add peppers and onions to skillet sprayed with non-stick cooking spray and stir over medium heat. Add 2 tablespoons Italian dressing and continue to stir until peppers and onions are tender.

Pour a little Italian dressing on each bagel half. Top with turkey and add peppers and onions. Place cheese on next and place top on sandwich. Warm in microwave oven 1 minute to melt cheese and serve warm.

Recipe makes 1 serving.

Grams of Fat Per Serving	Calories Per Serving
4	365

Ultra Lowfat

TORTILLA CASSEROLE
One of my best!

2   small onions, chopped
1   16-oz. can fat-free refried beans
1   lb. ground turkey breast
1   1¼-oz. pkg. taco seasoning
½   c. water
1   10-oz. can Campbell's 97% fat-free cream of
       mushroom soup
1   4-oz. can chopped green chilies
½   c. fat-free sour cream
½   c. fat-free cheese, grated
1   c. crushed no-oil tortilla chips

Preheat Oven: 350°

Combine 1 chopped onion with refried beans and line
bottom of 9" × 13" casserole with mixture.

Brown meat in skillet sprayed with nonstick cooking
spray. Add taco seasoning and stir. Add water and stir.
Add cream of mushroom soup and green chilies and
remove from heat. Add sour cream and mix thoroughly.

Pour mixture over refried beans. Add 1 chopped onion.
Sprinkle on grated cheese and top with tortilla chips.
Bake at 350° for 25–35 minutes.

Recipe makes 9 servings.

Grams of Fat Per Serving	Calories Per Serving
2	211

Ultra Lowfat

CAULIFLOWER AND BROCCOLI STIR-FRY
Italian style

1½ c. cauliflower pieces
1½ c. broccoli pieces
3 green onions, chopped
1 c. (¼ lb.) fresh mushrooms, sliced
salt to taste
¾ c. fat-free Italian dressing
2 t. grated orange peel

In large skillet sprayed with nonstick cooking spray, stir-fry cauliflower, broccoli, onions, and mushrooms over medium heat 4–5 minutes. Add small amount of water (¼ to ½ cup); cover and simmer 1–2 minutes. Remove lid and cook until most of the liquid is absorbed. Add salt, dressing, and orange peel and stir. Serve immediately.

Recipe makes 2 servings.

Grams of Fat Per Serving	Calories Per Serving
Less than 1 gram	82

Ultra Lowfat

VEGETABLE FAJITAS
Wonderful

1 t. sesame seeds
1 large onion, sliced
1 bell pepper, sliced
1 small zucchini, sliced
1 small yellow squash, sliced
3 fresh green chilies, sliced lengthwise
1 c. ($\frac{1}{4}$ lb.) mushrooms, sliced
2 t. dry fajita seasoning
1 t. garlic salt
  black pepper to taste
$\frac{1}{2}$ c. fat-free cheese, shredded
6 small flour tortillas
  salsa (optional)

In large skillet sprayed with nonstick cooking spray, lightly brown sesame seeds. Add onion and brown. Add bell pepper, zucchini, squash, green chilies, mushrooms, fajita seasoning, garlic salt, and black pepper. Stir over medium heat just until vegetables are tender. DO NOT OVERCOOK! Stir in cheese just before serving. Spoon mixture on tortillas and roll. Garnish with salsa if desired.

Recipe makes 6 servings.

Grams of Fat Per Serving	Calories Per Serving
1.5	155

SALMON CAKES
Easy and delicious

Salmon Cakes:

1   6⅛-oz. can salmon, drained
2   T. chopped onion
2   egg whites, slightly beaten
2   t. lemon juice
½   t. seasoned salt (optional)
    black pepper to taste
¼   c. fat-free cracker crumbs
½   c. cornmeal

In medium bowl, combine salmon, onion, egg whites, lemon juice, salt, pepper, and cracker crumbs and mix thoroughly. Form into patties and roll in cornmeal. Cook in skillet sprayed with nonstick cooking spray over medium to low heat 5–6 minutes on each side or until brown. Pour white sauce over and serve.

White Sauce:

½ c. evaporated skim milk
½ c. skim milk
2 t. Molly McButter
1 t. dill weed
1 T. lemon juice
  salt and black pepper to taste
2 T. flour

In small saucepan, combine all ingredients except flour. Use a whisk to blend in flour and stir over medium heat until slightly thickened.

Recipe makes 3 servings.

Grams of Fat Per Serving	Calories Per Serving
5	265

CREAM CHEESE
CHICKEN SALAD POCKETS
Refreshing summer sandwich

½ lb. boneless, skinless chicken breasts, cut into
　　small pieces
　　garlic powder
　　black pepper
2　T. fat-free Italian salad dressing
1　large tomato, chopped into small chunks
1　medium cucumber, chopped into small chunks
5　green onions, thinly sliced
½　c. (4 oz.) Kraft fat-free cream cheese
1　clove garlic, pressed
½　t. seasoned salt (optional)
3　pita breads (cut in half to make 6 pockets)

Season chicken pieces lightly with garlic powder and black pepper. Brown in skillet sprayed with nonstick cooking spray. Add Italian dressing and simmer until chicken is done. Set aside to cool.

In large bowl, combine vegetables, cream cheese, garlic, and seasoned salt and mix thoroughly. Add cooked chicken and mix. Chill and serve in pita pockets.

Recipe makes 6 servings.

Grams of Fat Per Serving	Calories Per Serving
2	162

Ultra Lowfat

CRISPY BUTTERMILK CHICKEN

¾ c. lowfat buttermilk
½ t. garlic salt
2 cloves garlic, pressed
   black pepper to taste
4 boneless, skinless chicken breasts
2 c. corn flakes, crushed

Mix together buttermilk, garlic salt, garlic, and black pepper. Dip chicken breasts in mixture and roll in corn flakes. Bake on baking sheet sprayed with nonstick cooking spray at 350° for 25–35 minutes.

Recipe makes 4 servings.

Grams of Fat Per Serving	Calories Per Serving
4	260

TORTILLA SOUP
Fabulous—don't miss this one

2 boneless, skinless chicken breasts (8 oz. total),
   cut into small pieces
1 medium onion, chopped
1 stalk celery, chopped
2 14-oz. cans chicken broth, defatted
1 14$\frac{1}{2}$-oz. can stewed, chopped tomatoes
1 clove garlic, pressed
1 4-oz. can chopped green chilies
$\frac{1}{2}$ 1$\frac{1}{4}$-oz. pkg. dry taco seasoning
$\frac{1}{2}$ c. fat-free sour cream
6 corn tortillas, cut into 1" squares

Brown chicken pieces in large pot sprayed with nonstick cooking spray. Add onion and celery and continue to brown. Add all remaining ingredients except sour cream and tortillas and simmer 15 minutes.

Add sour cream and simmer 1–2 minutes. Add tortillas and simmer 1–2 minutes. Serve.

Recipe makes 6 servings.

Grams of Fat Per Serving	Calories Per Serving
3	235

WHITE CHILI

Good with corn bread on a cold night

1   16-oz. pkg. dry white beans
2   14-oz. cans chicken broth, defatted
1½ c. water
2   boneless, skinless chicken breasts (8 oz. total),
        cut into small pieces
1   medium onion, chopped
1   stalk celery, chopped
1   4-oz. can chopped green chilies
1   clove garlic, pressed
½   t. chili powder
     salt and pepper to taste
½   c. fat-free sour cream

Rinse beans and cover with water. Bring to boil; turn off heat and let stand 1 hour and drain. Add chicken broth and water and simmer.

In skillet sprayed with nonstick cooking spray, brown chicken pieces, onion, and celery. Add to beans along with all remaining ingredients except sour cream. Simmer 2–3 hours or until beans are done. Add sour cream just before serving.

Recipe makes 6 servings.

Grams of Fat Per Serving	Calories Per Serving
2.5	227

Ultra Lowfat

PASTA-VEGETABLE CASSEROLE

1   10-oz. can Campbell's 97% fat-free cream of
     mushroom soup
1   10¾-oz. can Campbell's 99% fat-free tomato soup
1   5-oz. can evaporated skim milk
1   c. grated fat-free cheese
     dash of Tabasco sauce
½   t. seasoned salt (optional)
     salt to taste
½   t. black pepper
1   yellow squash, diced
1   medium onion, chopped
1   T. chopped green pepper
2   c. (½ lb.) fresh mushrooms, sliced
6   c. cooked pasta

Preheat Oven: 350°

In large bowl, combine cream of mushroom soup,
tomato soup, and evaporated milk and mix with electric mixer until smooth. By hand, fold in cheese,
Tabasco sauce, seasoned salt, salt, and black pepper. Add squash, onion, green pepper, mushrooms,
and pasta and stir. Bake in large casserole sprayed
with nonstick cooking spray at 350° for 45–50 minutes.

Recipe makes 8 servings.

Grams of Fat Per Serving	Calories Per Serving
2.5	220

Ultra Lowfat

CHILLED CREAM CHEESE
VEGGIE PIZZA
So quick—so easy—tastes great

⅓ cup (3 oz.) Kraft fat-free cream cheese
¼ t. garlic powder
1 t. dry onion flakes
¼ t. seasoned salt
1 small Boboli pizza crust—single serving size
2 T. canned mushrooms, drained
1 T. chopped green pepper
1 green onion, chopped
5 slices cucumber
   garlic salt to taste
   seasoned salt to taste

In small bowl, combine cream cheese, garlic powder, onion flakes, and seasoned salt. Mix thoroughly and spread on pizza crust. Layer with vegetables and sprinkle with garlic salt and seasoned salt. Eat immediately or chill before serving; either way is delicious.

Recipe makes 1 serving.

Grams of Fat Per Serving	Calories Per Serving
4	221

CHICKEN MARSALA WITH ANGEL HAIR PASTA

One of my best—don't miss it

8   oz. dry angel hair pasta
4   boneless, skinless chicken breasts
    garlic powder
    black pepper

Sauce:

¼   c. marsala cooking wine (available at most grocery stores)
1½ c. chicken broth, defatted
1½ T. Molly McButter
1   t. dry onion flakes
1   clove garlic, pressed
¼   c. evaporated skim milk
1   c. (¼ lb.) fresh mushrooms, sliced
    black pepper to taste
1   T. cornstarch
¼   c. cold water

Prepare angel hair pasta according to package directions, using no oil.

Season chicken breasts lightly with garlic powder and black pepper. Cook in skillet sprayed with nonstick cooking spray until golden brown and done. Remove from skillet and set aside.

Pour cooking wine into skillet and stir over low heat 1 minute. Add chicken broth, Molly McButter, onion flakes, and garlic and stir 1 minute. Add evaporated milk and mushrooms and simmer and stir until mushrooms are done, 2–3 minutes. Add black pepper.

In small bowl, mix cornstarch and cold water until smooth. Add to skillet and stir until sauce thickens. Remove from heat.

Place mound of pasta on each plate. Place 1 chicken breast on each mound and pour equal parts of sauce over each. Serve and enjoy.

Recipe makes 4 servings.

Grams of Fat Per Serving	Calories Per Serving
4	409

Ultra Lowfat

PIZZA BURGER
Especially for Greg

1   lb. ground turkey breast or chicken breast
½   bell pepper, sliced
1   medium onion, sliced
2   c. (½ lb.) fresh mushrooms, sliced
    garlic salt to taste
    black pepper to taste
6   lite hamburger buns
½   c. lowfat pizza sauce
1   c. fat-free mozzarella cheese, shredded

Form meat into 6 patties and brown and cook in skillet sprayed with nonstick cooking spray; season to taste and set aside.

In large skillet sprayed with nonstick cooking spray, brown and sauté bell pepper, onion, and mushrooms. Sprinkle with garlic salt and black pepper.

Assemble each burger with bun, meat patty, pizza sauce, cheese, and sautéed mixture. Place open-faced on baking sheet and place under broiler just long enough for sauce to heat and cheese to melt. Remove and place top bun on.

Recipe makes 6 servings.

Grams of Fat Per Serving	Calories Per Serving
3.5	184

Ultra Lowfat

BLACKENED ORANGE SHRIMP

Spicy and delicious

¾ c. orange juice concentrate
    grated peel from 1 orange
2 t. lite soy sauce
12 large shrimp
    blackened or Cajun spices to taste
    garlic salt to taste

Preheat Oven: 350°

In small bowl, combine orange juice concentrate, grated orange peel, and soy sauce.

Season both sides of shrimp heavily with blackened spices and lightly with garlic salt. Brown on each side in large skillet sprayed with nonstick cooking spray. Transfer to square or round baking dish sprayed with nonstick cooking spray and pour orange juice mixture on top. Bake at 350° for 30–35 minutes.

Recipe makes 4 servings.

Grams of Fat Per Serving	Calories Per Serving
1	152

SPICY OVEN CHICKEN

½ c. skim milk
1 t. lite soy sauce
½ t. Tabasco sauce
½ t. Worcestershire sauce
1 T. spicy hot mustard
1 clove garlic, pressed
¾ c. flour
    salt to taste
¼ t. black pepper
1 T. dry taco seasoning
4 boneless, skinless chicken breasts

Preheat Oven: 350°

In small bowl, mix milk, soy sauce, Tabasco sauce, Worcestershire sauce, mustard, and garlic. In another bowl, mix flour, salt, black pepper, and taco seasoning.

Dip chicken breasts in milk mixture and then in flour mixture and bake on baking sheet sprayed with non-stick cooking spray at 350° for 35–40 minutes. Spray top of chicken with small amount of butter-flavored nonstick spray.

Recipe makes 4 servings.

Grams of Fat Per Serving	Calories Per Serving
4	310

Ultra Lowfat

SPAGHETTI CASSEROLE
The best!

1   lb. ground turkey breast or chicken breast
1   medium onion, chopped
1½   c. (6 oz.) fresh mushrooms, sliced, sautéed
1   clove garlic, pressed
1   16-oz. can chopped tomatoes
1   8-oz. can tomato sauce
1   1⅓-oz. pkg. dry spaghetti sauce mix
1   8-oz. pkg. spaghetti, broken, cooked, and
        drained
½   c. fat-free mozzarella cheese, shredded
½   c. fat-free Parmesan cheese

Preheat Oven: 375°

Brown meat and onion in large skillet sprayed with nonstick cooking spray. Add mushrooms; simmer and stir 5 minutes. Add garlic, tomatoes, and tomato sauce and simmer 5 more minutes. Add spaghetti sauce mix and stir. Pour mixture over spaghetti and mix.

Pour half the mixture into large casserole sprayed with nonstick cooking spray. Sprinkle with mozzarella cheese and add remaining spaghetti mixture. Top with Parmesan and bake at 375° for 30–35 minutes.

Recipe makes 8 servings.

Grams of Fat Per Serving	Calories Per Serving
1.5	166

EGG FOO YUNG

½ c. carrots, shredded
2 green onions, chopped
2 c. bean sprouts
1 clove garlic, pressed
1½ c. fat-free liquid egg product
salt and black pepper to taste

Add carrots to large skillet sprayed with nonstick cooking spray and stir over medium heat 2–3 minutes. Add onions, bean sprouts, and garlic and remove from heat.

In large bowl, beat egg product with salt and black pepper. Add vegetable mixture and stir.

Spray skillet again with nonstick cooking spray. Using about ⅓ cup at a time, place mixture in skillet to form patties. Cook until egg is set, then turn and cook on other side. Repeat until all mixture is used.

Sauce:

1 c. canned vegetable broth
2 t. sugar
2 t. white vinegar
1 T. lite soy sauce
2 T. water
1 T. cornstarch

In small saucepan, heat broth, sugar, vinegar, and soy sauce. In small cup or bowl, stir together water and cornstarch. Add to saucepan and stir until thickened. Pour over Egg Foo Yung patties.

Recipe makes 6 servings.

Grams of Fat Per Serving	Calories Per Serving
1	62

Ultra Lowfat

CHICKEN GUMBO BURGERS

1   lb. ground chicken breast or turkey breast
½ medium onion, chopped
1   15-oz. can Healthy Choice chicken with rice soup
1   T. ketchup
1   T. mustard

In skillet sprayed with nonstick cooking spray, brown meat with onion. Add remaining ingredients and simmer over low heat 20–30 minutes. Serve on lite hamburger buns.

Recipe makes 6 servings.

Grams of Fat Per Serving	Calories Per Serving
2	141

Ultra Lowfat

SWEET ONION SANDWICH
Don't miss this one

Buttermist or other butter-flavored nonstick
    cooking spray
2 medium sweet Vidalia onions, sliced
    garlic salt to taste
    black pepper to taste
4 slices sourdough bread
2 slices fat-free Swiss cheese

Preheat Oven: 375°

In large skillet sprayed with nonstick cooking spray,
brown and sauté onions over medium heat until brown,
adding garlic salt and black pepper while cooking.

Spray 1 side of bread slices with nonstick cooking
spray and toast.

Place thick pile of cooked onions on 2 slices toast
and top each with 1 slice cheese. Warm at 375° long
enough to melt cheese. Top with bread slice and
serve warm.

Recipe makes 2 servings.

Grams of Fat Per Serving	Calories Per Serving
1	267

Ultra Lowfat

PASTA SALAD WITH HONEY MUSTARD CHICKEN

Sauce:

¼ c. honey
¼ c. spicy mustard
1 t. lemon juice
½ t. grated lemon peel
1 t. lite soy sauce
½ t. garlic salt

Salad:

4 boneless, skinless chicken breasts, cut into small pieces
salt and black pepper to taste
5 c. cooked pasta
1 14-oz. can artichoke hearts in water, drained and quartered
1 8-oz. bottle fat-free Italian dressing or fat-free honey-Dijon dressing

In small bowl, combine sauce ingredients and mix.

Brown chicken pieces in large skillet sprayed with non-stick cooking spray. While browning, add salt and pepper. Add sauce to browned chicken and simmer over low heat until most of sauce has been absorbed. Set aside to cool.

Combine pasta, artichoke hearts, and cooled chicken and toss. Add $\frac{1}{2}$ bottle dressing and chill. Add remaining dressing just before serving.

Recipe makes 6 servings.

Grams of Fat Per Serving	Calories Per Serving
4	357

Ultra Lowfat

HAM, CHEESE, AND ASPARAGUS ROLLS
Easy and delicious

¼ c. (2 oz.) Kraft fat-free cream cheese
½ t. garlic salt
⅛ t. black pepper
¼ cup fat-free Parmesan cheese
1½ t. horseradish
4   egg roll wrappers
4   slices Healthy Choice sliced ham
8   asparagus spears, cooked
4   slices Kraft fat-free Swiss cheese
1   egg white, slightly beaten
½ t. sesame seeds

Preheat Oven: 375°

In small bowl, combine cream cheese, garlic salt, black pepper, Parmesan, and horseradish. Stir and mix thoroughly.

Place 1 egg roll wrapper at a time on dinner plate and place 1 ham slice in center. Spread about 2 teaspoons cream cheese mixture in center of ham; then place 2 spears asparagus across ham and top with 1 slice cheese. Starting at corner, roll on the diagonal. On first roll, fold each end in toward center and continue rolling. Brush a little egg white on ends on last roll to hold it together.

Place finished rolls on baking sheet sprayed with non-stick cooking spray. Sprinkle sesame seeds on tops and bake at 375° for 15–20 minutes or until golden brown.

Recipe makes 4 servings.

Grams of Fat Per Serving	Calories Per Serving
1.5	152

BACON WITH BROWN SUGAR
So simple—so good

4   slices turkey bacon
¼ cup brown sugar

In nonstick skillet, brown turkey bacon on one side. Turn; sprinkle with brown sugar and continue cooking. Turn once more and cook slightly at medium heat. If heat is too high, sugar will scorch. Remove and serve. Do not put on paper towels to cool.

Recipe makes 2 servings.

Grams of Fat Per Serving	Calories Per Serving
4	170

Ultra Lowfat

TOSTADAS

6   small corn tortillas
     Buttermist or other butter-flavored nonstick
       cooking spray
     garlic salt
1   16-oz. can fat-free refried beans
½   c. fat-free sour cream
1   medium onion, chopped
1   c. fat-free cheese, grated
1   large tomato, chopped
2–3 c. chopped lettuce

Preheat Oven: 375°

Place tortillas on cookie sheet sprayed with nonstick cooking spray. Lightly spray tops of tortillas and sprinkle with garlic salt. Place another cookie sheet over top of tortillas so they will bake flat and not curl. Bake at 375° for 10–12 minutes. Remove and cool slightly.

Spread each tortilla with refried beans and sour cream and sprinkle tops with onion, cheese, tomato, and lettuce.

Recipe makes 6 servings.

Grams of Fat Per Serving	Calories Per Serving
2.5	235

Ultra Lowfat

SHRIMP ROCKEFELLER

1   T. lemon juice
1   T. flour
1   small onion, chopped
½ c. cooked spinach, chopped
1   T. parsley
2   t. Molly McButter
¼ c. fat-free liquid egg product
     salt and black pepper to taste
2   dozen medium shrimp, cooked and peeled
½ c. seasoned bread crumbs (look for lowest fat)

Preheat Oven: 350°

In small bowl, gradually add lemon juice to flour to make thin paste. Stir until smooth. Add onion, spinach, parsley, Molly McButter, egg product, salt, and pepper.

Spray medium casserole with nonstick cooking spray and line bottom with shrimp. Pour spinach mixture over top and sprinkle with bread crumbs. Bake at 350° for 15–20 minutes.

Recipe makes 6 servings.

Grams of Fat Per Serving	Calories Per Serving
1.5	131

Ultra Lowfat

SHRIMP FETTUCCINI WITH CREAMY CHEESE SAUCE

¾ c. evaporated skim milk
¾ c. skim milk
¾ c. (6 oz.) Kraft fat-free cream cheese
½ c. fat-free Parmesan cheese
1 T. Molly McButter
1 lb. cooked shrimp
   salt and black pepper to taste
4 c. fettuccini, cooked and drained

Preheat Oven: 350°

In food processor, combine evaporated milk, skim milk, cream cheese, Parmesan, and Molly McButter. Transfer to saucepan and stir over medium heat until smooth and warm. Add shrimp, salt, and pepper; stir and simmer 1–2 minutes. Serve over fettuccini.

Recipe makes 4 servings.

Grams of Fat Per Serving	Calories Per Serving
3	474

Ultra Lowfat

OVEN LEMON-PEPPER CHICKEN

¾ c. fat-free mayonnaise
1   clove garlic, pressed
1   T. fresh lemon juice
    grated peel from 1 lemon
4   boneless, skinless chicken breasts
1½ c. crushed corn flakes
    black pepper to taste

Preheat Oven: 350°

Mix together mayonnaise, garlic, lemon juice, and lemon peel. Dip and coat chicken breasts in mixture and roll in crushed corn flakes. Place on baking sheet sprayed with nonstick cooking spray and sprinkle with black pepper. Bake at 350° for 25–30 minutes.

Recipe makes 4 servings.

Grams of Fat Per Serving	Calories Per Serving
4	343

Ultra Lowfat

BLACKENED CHICKEN PASTA
Spicy and hot

2   boneless, skinless chicken breasts, cut into bite-
      size pieces
½ c. fat-free Italian dressing
1   clove garlic, pressed
      blackened or Cajun spices
4   c. cooked pasta
1   14-oz. can water-packed artichoke hearts, drained

Marinate chicken pieces in combined Italian dressing
and garlic about 1 hour; discard marinade.

Season chicken pieces heavily with blackened spices
and brown in skillet sprayed with nonstick cooking
spray over low heat until done. Cool.

Combine chicken, pasta, and artichoke hearts. Serve
with favorite dressing.

Recipe makes 4 servings.

Grams of Fat Per Serving	Calories Per Serving
2	353

Ultra Lowfat

CHICKEN WITH LEMON CREAM SAUCE
Absolutely wonderful

4   boneless, skinless chicken breasts
     garlic salt to taste
     black pepper to taste
1   c. chicken broth, defatted
1½ T. fresh lemon juice
1   t. grated lemon peel
¼   c. fat-free Parmesan cheese
⅓   c. fat-free sour cream
1   T. flour

Season chicken breasts with garlic salt and black pepper. In skillet sprayed with nonstick cooking spray, brown and cook over medium heat until done, 4–5 minutes each side.

In medium saucepan, combine chicken broth, lemon juice, lemon peel, Parmesan, and sour cream. Use whisk to stir until smooth. Add 2–3 tablespoons mixture to flour to make thin paste. Add paste back into sauce and stir over medium heat until thickened. Pour over chicken breasts and serve.

Recipe makes 4 servings.

Grams of Fat Per Serving	Calories Per Serving
4	356

Ultra Lowfat

ROCKEFELLER CASSEROLE

2 slices turkey bacon
1 medium onion, chopped
1 10-oz. box frozen spinach, thawed and drained
3 medium yellow crookneck squash, diced
4 c. Kellogg's stuffing mix croutons
½ c. fat-free liquid egg product
1 14-oz. can chicken broth, defatted
  salt and black pepper to taste

Preheat Oven: 325°

Brown and cook turkey bacon in nonstick skillet. Cool and crumble. Add onion to skillet and brown over medium heat.

Combine all ingredients and mix. Bake in large casserole sprayed with nonstick cooking spray at 325° for 45 minutes.

Recipe makes 8 servings.

Grams of Fat Per Serving	Calories Per Serving
3	266

Ultra Lowfat

PASTA PRIMAVERA
Really, really good

1   c. fresh broccoli pieces
1   c. carrots, sliced
1   c. zucchini, sliced
1½ c. (6 oz.) fresh mushrooms, sliced
1   large tomato, chopped
1   c. fresh snow peas
4   c. linguine noodles, cooked (8 oz. uncooked)

Steam or sauté vegetables and set aside while preparing sauce.

Sauce:

½ c. evaporated skim milk
1 c. skim milk
¾ c. chicken broth, defatted
½ c. fat-free sour cream
½ c. fat-free Parmesan cheese
3 cloves garlic, pressed
2 t. Molly McButter
   salt and black pepper to taste
2 T. flour

Combine all sauce ingredients except flour. Combine
small amount of mixture with flour to make thin paste.
Pour back into sauce and stir over medium heat until
slightly thickened.

Pour vegetables over noodles and pour sauce over
top. Toss and serve warm.

Recipe makes 8 servings.

Grams of Fat Per Serving	Calories Per Serving
2	187

Ultra Lowfat

BREAKFAST PIZZAS
These are great

½ pkg. (6-oz.) turkey sausage
4 slices turkey bacon
1 10-oz. can Campbell's 97% fat-free cream of
  mushroom soup
¼ c. skim milk
½ green or red pepper, chopped
¼ c. onion, chopped
1 8-oz. carton fat-free liquid egg product
2 T. Kraft fat-free cream cheese
  salt and black pepper to taste
1 7½-oz. can refrigerated no-fat biscuits
1 c. fat-free cheddar cheese, shredded

Preheat Oven: 375°

Cook turkey sausage in skillet; drain and set aside.
Cook turkey bacon in skillet or microwave; crumble
and set aside. Combine mushroom soup with milk
and set aside. In skillet sprayed with nonstick cooking spray, sauté pepper and onion until tender an
set aside.

Combine egg product and cream cheese and cook
until not quite done in skillet sprayed with nonstick
cooking spray. Remove from heat and add green pepper, onion, sausage, bacon, salt, and pepper.

Spray cookie sheet with nonstick cooking spray. Press each biscuit onto cookie sheet to make 4" circle. Place large spoonful of egg mixture on each and top with large spoonful of soup mixture. Sprinkle with shredded cheese. Bake at 375° for 10–12 minutes.

Recipe makes 8 servings.

Grams of Fat Per Serving	Calories Per Serving
7	208

Ultra Lowfat

CREAMY CHICKEN AND ARTICHOKE HEARTS OVER NOODLES

4   boneless, skinless chicken breasts
2   14-oz. cans chicken broth, defatted
     celery, carrot, and onion, chopped (seasoning for
       broth)
1   12-oz. can evaporated skim milk
½   c. chicken broth, defatted
¼   c. flour
3   slices fat-free cheddar cheese
3   slices fat-free Swiss cheese
½   t. caynne pepper
     salt to taste
1   4-oz. can button mushrooms, drained
1   14-oz. can artichoke hearts, drained and quartered
½   c. fat-free sour cream
1   clove garlic, pressed
½   12-oz. pkg. No Yolk noodles, cooked and drained

Preheat Oven: 350°

Simmer chicken breasts until tender in chicken broth
seasoned with celery, carrot, and onion. Cut chicken
into pieces and set aside. Reserve ½ cup chicken
broth and discard celery, carrot, and onion.

In saucepan, combine evaporated milk, reserved ½ cup chicken broth, and flour. Whisk until smooth and cook over low heat, stirring constantly, until thickened.

Cut cheeses into small pieces and add to sauce, stirring until melted. Add chicken, seasonings, mushrooms, artichoke hearts, sour cream, and garlic. Bake in casserole sprayed with nonstick cooking spray at 350° for 20 minutes. Serve over noodles.

Recipe makes 4 servings.

Grams of Fat Per Serving	Calories Per Serving
4	654

Ultra Lowfat

SANTA FE PIZZA

One of my best—don't miss it

Sauce:

2   T. chicken broth, defatted
1½ t. Molly McButter
1   clove garlic, pressed
2   T. fresh sweet basil, finely chopped

Pizza:

1   small Boboli pizza crust (single serving size)
1   small fresh green chili, sliced
2   T. fat-free Parmesan cheese
3   oz. boneless, skinless chicken breasts, cooked
        and cut into strips (charcoal grilled if possible)
2   slices sweet Vidalia onion
¼   c. fat-free mozzarella cheese, shredded

Preheat Oven: 400°

Combine sauce ingredients and brush on pizza crust.
Layer with green chili, Parmesan, chicken strips, onion,
and mozzarella cheese. Bake on baking sheet sprayed
with nonstick cooking spray at 400° for 12–15 minutes.

Recipe makes 2 servings.

Grams of Fat Per Serving	Calories Per Serving
2	150

Ultra Lowfat

CHICKEN BREAST MARINADE
Spicy and sweet

½ t. sesame seeds
¼ c. orange juice concentrate
1 T. lemon juice
4 T. lite soy sauce
3 green onions, chopped
2 t. fresh ginger root, grated
1 t. red pepper flakes
4 boneless, skinless chicken breasts

Brown sesame seeds over medium-low heat in small pan sprayed with nonstick cooking spray. In shallow bowl, combine remaining ingredients except chicken and mix. Add sesame seeds.

Marinate chicken breasts in mixture 30–60 minutes in refrigerator, turning occasionally. Cook in oven or charcoal on outdoor grill. Discard remaining marinade.

Recipe makes 4 servings.

Grams of Fat Per Serving	Calories Per Serving
4	312

HOT BROWN SANDWICH

Wonderful hot sandwich

Sauce:

1	small onion, chopped
3	T. flour
½	c. evaporated skim milk
1½	c. skim milk
¼	c. fat-free Parmesan cheese
¼	c. fat-free cheddar cheese, shredded
	salt and black or white pepper to taste

In large skillet sprayed with nonstick cooking spray, sauté onion until transparent. Add flour, evaporated milk, and skim milk and whisk until smooth. Cook over medium heat until sauce begins to thicken. Add cheeses and continue stirring over heat until well blended. Add salt and pepper and remove from heat.

Topping:

2	c. (½ lb.) fresh sliced mushrooms
4	slices turkey bacon

In large skillet sprayed with nonstick cooking spray, sauté mushrooms until tender. Cook and crumble turkey bacon.

Sandwich Base:

8   slices lowfat bread, toasted
8   slices turkey breast

Prepare each sandwich in small oven-proof individual serving dishes. In each dish, place 1 slice of toast. Cover with 2 slices turkey breast; then spoon cheese sauce over each. Place under broiler until sauce begins to bubble. Cut remaining toast diagonally and place at each end of sandwich. Top with mushrooms and bacon and serve while hot.

Recipe makes 4 sandwiches.

Grams of Fat Per Serving	Calories Per Serving
3	400

Ultra Lowfat

VEGETARIAN ENCHILADAS
Wonderful

1   carrot, sliced
½   c. chicken broth, defatted
1½ c. (6 oz.) fresh mushrooms, sliced
1   small zucchini, sliced
1   small yellow squash, sliced
1   medium onion, sliced
2   fresh green chilies, sliced
1   T. fresh cilantro, chopped
1   1¼-oz. pkg. dry taco seasoning
½   t. garlic salt
1   clove garlic, pressed
1   medium tomato, chopped
6   small fat-free flour tortillas

Topping:

⅓   c. evaporated skim milk
½   c. shredded fat-free mozzarella cheese
2   green onions (including tops), chopped
½   t. garlic salt

Preheat Oven: 350°

Add carrots and small amount of chicken broth to large skillet sprayed with nonstick cooking spray. Simmer and stir. Add mushrooms and simmer 2–3 minutes. Add zucchini, yellow squash, onion, green chilies, cilantro, taco seasoning, garlic salt, and garlic. Pour in a little more chicken broth and simmer and stir until vegetables are partially done. Add tomato. DO NOT OVERCOOK; leave some crunch in vegetables. Remove from heat and cool slightly.

Place about ½ cup mixture on each tortilla and roll; arrange in baking dish sprayed with nonstick cooking spray. Combine topping ingredients and pour over enchiladas. Bake at 350° for 25–30 minutes. Garnish with salsa or fat-free sour cream if desired.

Recipe makes 6 servings.

Grams of Fat Per Serving	Calories Per Serving
2.5	180

ORANGE MARMALADE CHICKEN
Delicious flavor

1   lb. boneless, skinless chicken breasts
½   t. Molly McButter
1   12-oz. jar sweet orange marmalade
⅓   c. chicken broth, defatted
1   4.3 oz. pkg. Lipton onion soup mix, dry
4   c. rice, cooked

Preheat Oven: 350°

Place chicken in 8" baking dish sprayed with nonstick cooking spray; sprinkle with Molly McButter.

In medium bowl, combine orange marmalade, chicken broth, and onion soup mix. Pour over chicken and bake at 350° for 45 minutes. Serve over rice.

Recipe makes 4 servings

Grams of Fat Per Serving	Calories Per Serving
4	634

Fat Free 2

PIES, PASTRIES, & DESSERTS

Ultra Lowfat

CHOCOLATE CHIP COOKIES

2¾ c. flour
1   t. baking soda
1   t. salt
1   c. unsweetened applesauce
¾   c. granulated sugar
¾   c. brown sugar
1   t. vanilla extract
½   c. Egg Beaters
1   12-oz. pkg. chocolate chips

Preheat Oven: 375°

In small bowl, combine flour, baking soda, and salt; set aside.

In large bowl, combine applesauce, sugars, vanilla, and Egg Beaters until well blended. Add flour mixture and stir until well blended. Stir in chocolate chips. Bake on ungreased cookie sheet at 375° for 9–11 minutes or until edges are golden brown.

Recipe makes 5 dozen cookies.
Serving size is 3 cookies

Grams of Fat Per Serving	Calories Per Serving
2	67

Recipe Contributed by: Janet Potts, R.D., L.D.
St. John Medical Center
Tulsa, Oklahoma

Ultra Lowfat

PUMPKIN CHEESECAKE
Really good

Crust:

8   graham cracker squares
2   T. sugar

Filling:

1   16-oz. can pumpkin
2   c. (16 oz.) fat-free cream cheese
1   c. fat-free sour cream
4   egg whites
$1\frac{1}{4}$ c. brown sugar
$1\frac{1}{2}$ T. pumpkin pie spice
$\frac{1}{4}$ t. salt
1   t. vanilla extract

Preheat Oven: 300°

In food processor, grind graham crackers and add 2 tablespoons sugar and process lightly. Sprinkle mixture evenly over bottom of large pie plate sprayed with nonstick cooking spray. Set aside.

In food processor, combine filling ingredients and process until well blended. Very carefully pour over crust, trying not to disturb crumbs. Bake at 300° for 55–60 minutes.

Recipe makes 8 servings.

Grams of Fat Per Serving	Calories Per Serving
1	208

Ultra Lowfat

ORANGE POPPY SEED CAKE
The best—wonderful

1 pkg. lowfat white cake mix
2 T. poppy seeds
¾ c. fat-free liquid egg product
1 c. fat-free sour cream
1 6-oz. can frozen orange juice concentrate
⅓ c. water
2 t. almond extract
½ t. cinnamon
2 T. sugar

Preheat Oven: 350°

In large bowl, combine all ingredients except cinnamon and sugar and beat with electric mixer 2 minutes.

Spray bundt pan with nonstick cooking spray. Combine sugar and cinnamon and sprinkle evenly over inside of pan. Pour in cake batter and bake at 350° for 45 minutes.

Recipe makes 12 servings.

Grams of Fat Per Serving	Calories Per Serving
3	255

Ultra Lowfat

HOMEMADE
STRAWBERRY ICE CREAM

½ c. fat-free sour cream
2⅓ c. sugar
1½ c. fat-free liquid egg product
2   10-oz. pkgs. frozen strawberries with sugar
3   12-oz. cans evaporated skim milk
2   t. vanilla
⅛   t. salt
       enough skim milk to fill freezer container to fill
          line (about 1 quart)

In large bowl, combine sour cream, sugar, and egg product with electric mixer. Add remaining ingredients except skim milk and mix well. Pour into freezer container and add skim milk. Freeze according to freezer directions.

Recipe makes 16 servings.

Grams of Fat Per Serving	Calories Per Serving
Less than 1 gram	238

ALICE'S LEMON BARS
Absolutely divine

Cake:

1 pkg. lowfat white cake mix
1 3-oz. pkg. box lemon gelatin
¾ c. fat-free liquid egg product
⅔ c. lemon juice
⅔ c. water
   grated peel from 1 lemon

Glaze:

1½ c. powdered sugar
   juice of 2 lemons

Preheat Oven: 350°

Combine cake ingredients and beat with electric mixer 2 minutes. Pour into 11" × 14" pan sprayed with nonstick cooking spray and bake at 350° for 25–30 minutes.

In small bowl, combine powdered sugar and lemon juice and stir with spoon until smooth. Pour over warm cake. Cool and cut into squares.

Recipe makes 12 servings.

Grams of Fat Per Serving	Calories Per Serving
3	206

Recipe Contributed by: Alice Ann Williams

LEMON SOUR CREAM CAKE
Divine—one of my best

Cake:

1   pkg. lowfat white cake mix
¾ c. lemon juice
¾ c. water
1   c. fat-free sour cream
    grated peel from 1 lemon
1   3-oz. pkg. lemon gelatin
3   egg whites
½ t. lemon extract

Glaze:

1   c. powdered sugar
2   T. lemon juice

Preheat Oven: 350°

In large bowl, combine cake ingredients and mix with electric mixer. Bake in 9″ × 13″ glass baking dish sprayed with nonstick cooking spray at 350° for 40–45 minutes.

In small bowl, combine glaze ingredients and stir by hand until smooth. Pour over warm cake.

Recipe makes 12 servings.

Grams of Fat Per Serving	Calories Per Serving
3	241

Ultra Lowfat

ZESTY ORANGE CAKE

Fabulous—one of my best

Cake:

1	pkg. lowfat white cake mix
3	egg whites
1	c. orange juice
⅓	c. lemon juice
	grated peel from 1 orange
1	c. fat-free sour cream
1	t. orange extract

Glaze:

1	cup powdered sugar
1½	T. orange juice concentrate
1	T. lemon juice
1	t. grated orange peel

Preheat Oven: 350°

In large bowl, combine cake ingredients and mix with electric mixer until thoroughly blended. Bake in 9" × 13" cake pan sprayed with nonstick cooking spray (use glass baking dish if possible) at 350° for 40–45 minutes.

In small bowl, combine glaze ingredients; stir by hand until smooth. Pour over warm cake.

Recipe makes 12 servings.

Grams of Fat Per Serving	Calories Per Serving
3	261

Fat Free

STRAWBERRY DREAM
Totally fat free and out of this world

Topping:

1½ (12-oz.) Kraft fat-free cream cheese
⅓ c. sugar
⅓ c. fat-free sour cream
1 t. vanilla extract

Suggestions for Shortcake:

fat-free pound cake
angel -food cake
lowfat biscuits (add a little sugar to lowfat biscuit
mix)

2 10-oz. pkgs. frozen sliced strawberries with
sugar

Combine topping ingredients and stir until smooth.

For each serving, place shortcake on serving dish. Add
several spoonfuls of strawberries and top with a few
spoonfuls of topping. Enjoy.

Recipe makes 6 large servings.

Grams of Fat Per Serving	Calories Per Serving
0 (with fat-free pound cake)	452

Fat Free

OLD-FASHIONED TAPIOCA PUDDING
Rich and creamy

2   c. evaporated skim milk
1   c. skim milk
½   c. sugar
3½ T. minute tapioca
¼   c. fat-free liquid egg product
1   t. Molly McButter
1   t. vanilla extract

In medium saucepan, combine all ingredients except vanilla; stir and let stand 5 minutes.

Stir over medium heat until mixture comes to boil. Remove from heat and add vanilla. Let cool 15–20 minutes. Mixture will thicken as it cools. Serve warm or chilled.

Recipe makes 6 servings.

Grams of Fat Per Serving	Calories Per Serving
0	168

Fat Free

LEMON CHEESECAKE
Made with Kraft fat-free cream cheese

Crust:

8   graham cracker squares, ground
2   T. sugar
2   t. Molly McButter

Filling:

1   c. fat-free sour cream
3   8-oz. cartons Kraft fat-free cream cheese*
5   egg whites
1   c. sugar
4   T. fresh lemon juice (about 2 lemons)
    grated peel from 1 lemon
¼   t. salt
2   T. flour

Preheat Oven: 350°

In small bowl, combine crust ingredients and mix. Sprinkle evenly over bottom and a little on sides of 10" pie plate sprayed with nonstick cooking spray; set aside.

In food processor, combine filling ingredients and

process until thoroughly blended. Very gently pour over crust. Bake at 350° for 20 minutes. Reduce temperature to 225° and bake additional 1 hour and 10 minutes. Remove from oven and cool.

Pie must be refrigerated several hours or overnight before slicing and serving.

Recipe makes 8 servings.

*This recipe will turn out entirely different with other brands of fat-free cream cheese. Use only Kraft fat-free cream cheese for this recipe.

Grams of Fat Per Serving	Calories Per Serving
0	307

LEMON CHESS PIE
Wonderful

Crust:

½ c. Pioneer Low-Fat Biscuit Mix*
1 T. sugar
1 t. Molly McButter

Filling:

1½ c. evaporated skim milk
1 c. fat-free liquid egg product
2 t. Molly McButter
½ c. plus 3 T. sugar
   juice from 2 lemons
   grated peel from 1 lemon
1 t. vanilla extract

Preheat Oven: 300°

In small bowl, combine crust ingredients and stir. Sprinkle evenly over bottom of 9" pie plate sprayed with nonstick cooking spray and set aside.

In food processor, combine filling ingredients and

process. Pour very gently over crust mixture, trying not to disturb crust. Bake at 300° for 55–60 minutes. Cool and serve.

Recipe makes 8 servings.

*If you can't find Pioneer Low-Fat Biscuit Mix in your area, use a light biscuit mix; however, this will add a few grams of fat to each serving.

Grams of Fat Per Serving	Calories Per Serving
Less than 1 gram	168

Fat Free

PINEAPPLE CREAM PIE

Don't miss this one—absolutely one of my best!

Crust:

½ c. Grape Nuts cereal
2½ T. sugar
½ t. Molly McButter

Filling:

¾   c. fat-free liquid egg product
1¼ c. sugar
⅓   c. flour
⅓   c. (3 oz.) Kraft fat-free cream cheese
1   T. Molly McButter
1   t. vanilla extract
1   15¼-oz. can crushed pineapple in its own juice
      (pour off juice but do not squeeze all the liquid
      out)

Preheat Oven: 325°

Pour Grape Nuts over bottom of 9" pie plate sprayed with nonstick cooking spray. Sprinkle 2½ tablespoons sugar and ½ teaspoon Molly McButter evenly over Grape Nuts and set aside.

In medium bowl and using electric mixer, cream together all ingredients for fillling except pineapple until smooth. Fold in pineapple with spoon. Carefully pour over crust, trying not to disturb Grape Nuts. Bake at 325° for 50–55 minutes.

Recipe makes 8 servings.

Grams of Fat Per Serving	Calories Per Serving
0	259

Fat Free

PEACH COBBLER
Yummy

Filling:

4   c. frozen or fresh peaches
¾ c. sugar
1   t. lemon juice
1   t. Molly McButter

Crust:

1½ c. Pioneer Low-Fat Biscuit Mix*
1¼ c. evaporated skim milk
2   T. sugar

Preheat Oven: 350°

Combine filling ingredients. Stir gently until sugar starts to dissolve and set aside.

Combine biscuit mix and evaporated milk and stir until well blended. Mixture will be like thin batter. Add sugar and mix.

Pour half the batter into 9" × 13" baking dish sprayed with nonstick cooking spray. Spoon fruit mixture evenly over top. Pour remaining batter evenly over top of peaches. Sprinkle spoonful of granulated sugar over top. Bake at 350° for 30 minutes. Serve hot or cold.

Recipe makes 8 servings.

*If you can't find Pioneer Low-Fat Biscuit Mix in your area, use a light biscuit mix; however, this will add a few grams of fat to each serving.

Grams of Fat Per Serving	Calories Per Serving
Less than 1 gram	266

Ultra Lowfat

CUSTARD PIE
Makes its own crust—this one is great

Crust:

½ c. Pioneer Low-Fat Biscuit Mix*
1 t. Molly McButter
1 T. sugar

Filling:

1 c. fat-free liquid egg product
½ c. plus 1 T. sugar
1 c. evaporated skim milk
1 c. skim milk
2 t. Molly McButter
1 t. vanilla extract
¼ t. nutmeg

Preheat Oven: 300°

In small bowl, combine ingredients for crust. Sprinkle over bottom of large pie plate sprayed with nonstick cooking spray. Smooth with spoon to even out mixture over entire bottom. Set aside.

In food processor, combine filling ingredients and mix well. Very carefully pour into pie plate, trying not to disturb crust. Bake at 300° for 45–55 minutes or until center is set.

Recipe makes 8 servings.

*If you can't find Pioneer Low-Fat Biscuit Mix in your area, use a light biscuit mix; however, this will add a few grams of fat to each serving.

Grams of Fat Per Serving	Calories Per Serving
Less than 1 gram	83

CHOCOLATE CHIP PIE

This one is the best yet!

Crust:
—————

½ c. Grape Nuts cereal
2½ T. sugar
½ t. Molly McButter

Filling:
—————

1   c. fat-free liquid egg product
1⅓ c. sugar
⅓ c. flour
1½ T. Molly McButter
1   t. vanilla extract
¼ t. almond extract
⅓ c. fat-free sour cream
⅓ c. regular-size semisweet chocolate chips
⅓ c. miniature semisweet chocolate chips

Preheat Oven: 325°

Sprinkle Grape Nuts evenly over bottom of 9" pie plate sprayed with nonstick cooking spray. Sprinkle evenly with 2½ tablespoons sugar and ½ teaspoon Molly McButter and set aside.

In medium bowl, using mixer, combine egg product, sugar, flour, Molly McButter, vanilla and almond extracts, and sour cream. Cream until smooth. Gently pour slowly over Grape Nuts, trying not to disturb crust.

Using the regular-size chocolate chips, take a few at a time and drop each chip on top of filling, then fill in various places until all chips are used. These will gradually sink into filling. Sprinkle miniature chips on top for garnish. Bake at 325° for 50 minutes.

Recipe makes 8 servings.

Grams of Fat Per Serving	Calories Per Serving
4.5	294

Fat Free

CHOCOLATE CHEESECAKE

Made with Kraft fat-free cream cheese

Crust:

8 graham cracker squares, ground
2 T. sugar
2 t. Molly McButter

Filling:

1 c. fat-free sour cream
3 8-oz. cartons Kraft fat-free cream cheese*
5 egg whites
1 c. sugar
2 T. Hershey's cocoa powder
2 t. fresh lemon juice
$\frac{1}{4}$ t. salt
2 T. flour

Preheat Oven: 350°

In small bowl, mix crust ingredients and sprinkle evenly over bottom of 10" pie plate sprayed with nonstick cooking spray. Set aside.

In food processor, combine filling ingredients and process until thoroughly blended. Very gently pour over crust.

Bake at 350° for 20 minutes; reduce temperature to 225° and bake additional 1 hour and 10 minutes. Cool.

Pie must be refrigerated several hours or overnight before slicing and serving.

Recipe makes 8 servings.

*This recipe will turn out entirely different with other brands of fat-free cream cheese. Use only Kraft fat-free cream cheese for this recipe.

Grams of Fat Per Serving	Calories Per Serving
0	327

Fat Free

CHERRY SOUR CREAM CAKE

1½ c. fat-free liquid egg product
½ c. fat-free cottage cheese
1 c. fat-free sour cream
1 T. Molly McButter
1 t. vanilla extract
1 c. sugar
2 c. Pioneer Low-Fat Biscuit Mix*
1 21-oz. can cherry pie filling

Preheat Oven: 350°

Combine egg product, cottage cheese, sour cream, Molly McButter, vanilla, and sugar and beat with electric mixer 1–2 minutes.

Add biscuit mix and mix thoroughly. FOLD in pie filling (do not mix). Pour mixture into 7" × 11" baking dish sprayed with nonstick cooking spray. Bake at 350° for 45 minutes.

Recipe makes 12 servings.

*If you can't find Pioneer Low-Fat Biscuit Mix in your area, use a light biscuit mix; however, this will add a few grams of fat to each serving.

Grams of Fat Per Serving	Calories Per Serving
Less than 1 gram	181

Fat Free

OLD-FASHIONED BLACKBERRY COBBLER
One of my best! Don't miss it!

Filling:

4   c. frozen blackberries, thawed
¾   c. sugar
1   t. lemon juice
1   t. Molly McButter

Crust:

1½ c. Pioneer Low-Fat Biscuit Mix*
1¼ c. evaporated skim milk
¼   c. sugar

Preheat Oven: 350°

Combine filling ingredients. Stir gently until sugar starts to dissolve and set aside.

Combine biscuit mix and milk and stir until well blended. Mixture will be like thin batter. Add sugar and mix.

Pour half the batter into 9" × 13" baking dish sprayed with nonstick cooking spray. Spoon berry mixture evenly over top. Pour remaining batter evenly over berries. Sprinkle spoonful of granulated sugar over top. Bake at 350° for 30 minutes. Serve hot or cold.

Recipe makes 8 servings.

*If you can't find Pioneer Low-Fat Biscuit Mix in your area, use a light biscuit mix; however, this will add a few grams of fat to each serving.

Grams of Fat Per Serving	Calories Per Serving
Less than 1 gram	278

BANANA CREAM PUDDING

Awesome

Bottom Layer:

⅓ cup graham cracker crumbs
3   T. sugar
2   t. Molly McButter

Filling:

1   3-oz. pkg. (not instant) vanilla pudding and pie
    filling mix
1½ cups evaporated skim milk
½   cup skim milk
⅓   cup sugar
1   t. Molly McButter
½   t. vanilla extract
⅓   cup fat-free sour cream
3   large bananas, sliced

Topping:

¼   cup graham cracker crumbs
2   T. sugar

In small bowl, combine ingredients for bottom layer and sprinkle evenly over bottom of 9" pie plate sprayed with nonstick cooking spray. Set aside.

In medium saucepan, combine pudding mix, evaporated milk, skim milk, sugar, and Molly McButter. Stir over medium heat until pudding comes to a boil. Remove from heat and add vanilla and sour cream. Mix with electric mixer until smooth and creamy. Add sliced bananas and spoon mixture into pie plate.

Combine ingredients for topping and sprinkle over top. Chill to set.

Recipe makes 8 servings.

Grams of Fat Per Serving	Calories Per Serving
Less than 1 gram	243

Ultra Lowfat

NOODLE PUDDING

If you like custard or rice pudding, you'll love this

1 8-oz. pkg. No Yolk noodles
1 t. Molly McButter
¾ c. sugar
1 c. fat-free cottage cheese
1 cup fat-free sour cream
1 c. (8-oz.) Kraft fat-free cream cheese, softened
½ t. salt
2 t. vanilla extract
1¼ c. fat-free liquid egg product
½ c. raisins (optional)
   cinnamon

Preheat Oven: 350°

In large saucepan, cook noodles in boiling water until tender, 8–10 minutes. Drain and set aside.

In large bowl, beat together Molly McButter, sugar, cottage cheese, sour cream, cream cheese, salt, vanilla, egg product, and raisins. Stir in noodles.

Pour into 13" × 9" baking dish sprayed with nonstick cooking spray and sprinkle with cinnamon. Bake at 350° for 45–50 minutes. Let stand 5 minutes before cutting. Serve warm or cold.

Recipe makes 10 servings.

Grams of Fat Per Serving	Calories Per Serving
1	258

Fat Free

FANCY RICE PUDDING DESSERT

¾ c. (6 oz.) Kraft fat-free cream cheese
⅓ c. fat-free sour cream
½ c. sugar
½ t. vanilla extract
2 c. cooked rice
1 6-oz. jar maraschino cherries, drained
1 8-oz. can crushed pineapple, drained
1½ c. miniature marshmallows

Cream together cream cheese, sour cream, sugar, and vanilla.

Combine remaining ingredients; pour over cream cheese mixture and stir. Chill and serve.

Recipe makes 8 servings.

Grams of Fat Per Serving	Calories Per Serving
0	234

Ultra Lowfat

PECAN PIE
You won't believe how good this is with NO pecans!

Crust:

2   large fat-free flour tortillas
    Buttermist or other butter-flavored nonstick
        cooking spray
½ t. Molly McButter

Preheat Oven: 350°

Place 1 tortilla in 9" pie plate sprayed with nonstick cooking spray. Spray tortilla and sprinkle with Molly McButter. Place second tortilla on top and spray lightly with butter spray. Using another 9" pie plate, spray outside bottom and place on top of tortillas. This helps press and form pie crust. Bake crust with pie plate on top at 350° for 7 minutes. Remove extra pie plate, cool slightly while preparing filling.

Filling:

¾ c. fat-free liquid egg product
½ c. light corn syrup
1 c. brown sugar
1 t. flour
1 T. Molly McButter
1 t. vanilla extract
⅓ c. Grape Nuts cereal

In large bowl, combine all ingredients except Grape Nuts and mix with electric mixer. Pour into partially baked crust. Sprinkle Grape Nuts over top of filling, and bake at 350° for 35 minutes. DO NOT cook over 35 minutes or it might spill over sides while baking. Also, do not worry about how it looks while cooking because it will puff up high but will go back down as soon as it cools.

Recipe makes 8 servings.

Grams of Fat Per Serving	Calories Per Serving
1.5	247

Ultra Lowfat

STRAWBERRY CREAM CHEESE PIE
Wonderful

Crust:

2   large fat-free flour tortillas
    Buttermist or other butter-flavored nonstick
      cooking spray
½ t. Molly McButter

Preheat Oven: 350°

Place 1 tortilla in deep 9½" pie plate sprayed with non-stick cooking spray. Spray tortilla lightly with butter spray and sprinkle with Molly McButter. Place second tortilla on top and spray lightly with butter spray. Spray outside bottom of another empty pie plate and set it down inside and on top of tortillas for baking. Bake at 350° for 13 minutes. Remove and cool; remove extra pie plate. Cool thoroughly before adding filling.

Filling:

1   envelope Knox unflavored gelatin
½   c. hot water
1   16-oz. pkg. frozen strawberries with sugar,
       thawed
1½ (12-oz.) Kraft fat-free cream cheese
⅓   c. sugar

Stir gelatin into hot water until dissolved. Combine with remaining ingredients in food processor and mix. Pour into prepared crust.

Topping:

½   envelope Knox unflavored gelatin
½   c. hot water
1½ c. fat-free sour cream
⅓   c. sugar
½   t. vanilla extract

Stir gelatin into hot water until dissolved. Combine with remaining ingredients and mix with electric mixer. Pour gently over filling. Chill several hours or overnight.

Recipe makes 10 servings.

Grams of Fat Per Serving	Calories Per Serving
1	237

Ultra Lowfat

CARAMEL APPLE CAKE
Heavy, moist, and wonderful

Cake:

2   large apples
2½ c. flour
½   t. baking soda
2   t. baking powder
1½ t. cinnamon
2   T. Molly McButter
1½ c. sugar
½   c. fat-free liquid egg product
½   c. fat-free sour cream
3   pitted prunes
¾   c. evaporated skim milk
4   T. fat-free caramel ice cream topping

Topping:

¼   c. oatmeal
⅓   c. brown sugar
5–6 T. fat-free caramel ice cream topping

Preheat Oven: 350°

Peel and finely chop apples and set aside. Stir or sift together flour, baking soda, baking powder, cinnamon, and Molly McButter until thoroughly mixed.

In food processor, combine sugar, egg product, sour cream, prunes, and milk. Process until smooth. Pour mixture over apples and stir.

Using electric mixer, gradually add flour mixture to apple mixture and blend until all flour has been added. Pour into 9" x 13" glass baking dish that has been sprayed with nonstick cooking spray. Drizzle 4 tablespoons caramel topping over top.

In small bowl, combine oatmeal and brown sugar and sprinkle over top of cake batter. Drizzle 5–6 tablespoons caramel topping over top. Bake at 350° for 45–50 minutes. Test center with toothpick for doneness.

Recipe makes 12 servings.

Grams of Fat Per Serving	Calories Per Serving
Less than 1 gram	274

CHOCOLATE-CHERRY
SOUR CREAM CAKE

Fabulous

1½ c. flour
⅓ c. dry cocoa
2   t. Molly McButter
1   c. sugar
1   c. water
¼ c. light corn syrup
1   t. vanilla extract
½ c. fat-free sour cream
½ t. vinegar
½ t. baking soda

Preheat Oven: 350°

In large bowl, combine flour, cocoa, and Molly McButter; mix thoroughly.

Using electric mixer, combine sugar, water, corn syrup, vanilla, sour cream, vinegar, and baking soda. Mix until smooth. Add dry ingredients gradually. Pour in 9" × 13" baking dish sprayed with nonstick cooking spray.

Topping:

¾ c. fat-free sour cream
⅓ c. sugar
1 21-oz. can cherry pie filling

In small bowl, combine sour cream and sugar and mix until smooth. Drop pie filling by spoonfuls over top of cake batter and follow each spoonful with sour cream mixture. Bake at 350° for 45–50 minutes.

Recipe makes 12 servings.

Grams of Fat Per Serving	Calories Per Serving
Less than 1 gram	255

INDEX